The Sandpiper Trust

The Sandpiper Trust was founded in 2000 following the tragic death of Sandy Dickson who drowned, aged 14, in a remote lake whilst on holiday in Canada. The Trust gives emergency medical equipment in the form of life saving medical bags which it provides to GPs working or living in remote and rural Scotland.

The equipment is given to GPs who have undergone training in accident and emergency procedures with BASICS SCOTLAND (British Association of Immediate Care) who organise training courses throughout rural Scotland from their base at Sandpiper House, Auchterarder, Perthshire.

Both Sandpiper and BASICS aim to provide skilled medical care at the scenes of traumatic emergencies and sudden illnesses that occur in the countryside and in the rural workplace.

Accidents happen – lives are lost, both young and old, on the road, at sea, in the countryside and through tragic accidents or sudden illnesses in the home or garden.

It is widely acknowledged that if specialist medical care can be provided during The Golden Hour – the critical period between a serious accident or sudden illness and getting a patient to hospital – the chances of survival and recovery are significantly improved.

The added provision of Vehicle Locators to Sandpiper doctors allows the Ambulance Dispatch Centres to identify, within seconds, when there is a doctor nearby to an incident. Once alerted the doctor can attend the incident and perform life-saving procedures whilst the ambulance is *en route*.

The continuing provision of Sandpiper Bags together with essential training and vehicle locators means that in Scotland an increasing number of patients are arriving from rural communities at Accident and Emergency Departments fully resuscitated and pain free. Lives which might otherwise have been lost, have been saved – a true memorial to a Scottish country-loving lad!

The Sandpiper Cookbook

Dedicated to all those who work
in the world of emergency pre-hospital care
in remote and rural Scotland

And in memory of
Sandy Dickson
(1986-2000)

A note from our patron – Gavin Hastings OBE

When I was approached by the family of Sandy Dickson to help with a new Scottish charity – The Sandpiper Trust - I never imagined that so much would be achieved in such a short space of time.

This has been down to the enthusiasm of so many people who have worked tirelessly on behalf of Sandpiper including the originator of this idea, Claire Maitland. Her appetite for fundraising ideas knows no bounds and she has brought many people along with her on her crusade all of whom, like me, have been willing to follow. As a result hundreds of GPs throughout Scotland have been provided with essential emergency medical equipment with every pound raised helping to improve pre-hospital care and saving lives in rural Scotland.

The success of The Sandpiper Trust has arisen from the tremendous support from such a wide range of people throughout the country. The proof of the pudding (and this is a cookbook of course!) can be seen by the number of recipes provided from all corners of Scotland and beyond from people ranging from doctors to students to rugby players (who think they can cook!) to Gordon Ramsay (who as a former footballer certainly can cook!). May I thank all of the contributors for sharing their favourite recipes with you all and trust that many dinner table stories will be prompted as a result of you choosing them and enjoying them with your friends and family.

As well as recipes, The Sandpiper Cookbook has delicious cocktails (including Tiger Wood's exclusive wedding cocktail) and, more importantly, emergency medical tips which are essential for all of us. All proceeds raised from the sale of this cookbook will help continue the work and the success of The Sandpiper Trust.

The greatest satisfaction to me comes when I hear reports back from doctors of the lives that have been saved in incidents throughout Scotland as a direct result of the Sandpiper equipment that they have been given. I am therefore extremely grateful that as a result of you buying or having been given this cookbook we are in a small way helping to save yet more lives throughout this great country of ours.

Gavin Hastings OBE
PATRON OF THE SANDPIPER TRUST
FORMER CAPTAIN OF THE BRITISH LIONS AND SCOTLAND

The Sandpiper Cookbook
'...not just another charity cookbook'

We all have our own recipe books, often no more than a jumble of cuttings and jotted down notes. They are the recipes that have fired our imaginations, proved Godsends in times of culinary emergency or tickled the tastebuds of friends and family over the years.

Why then would you want to produce a book with recipes and emergency medical tips? There will be questions asked.

We asked many supporters of the Sandpiper Trust – friends and relations, doctors and nurses, rugby players and cricketers, students and even celebrity chefs – for their recipes to compile this cookbook. Yet, it is much more than just a cookbook.

With the advice of several Scottish doctors we have compiled a list of essential and non-essential items for the medical cabinet. If, on a cold, miserable Sunday morning in December, you succumb to a dreaded winter bug, you will be thankful to The Sandpiper Trust for encouraging you to restock your medicine cabinet. This will save you from having to drag yourself out of bed to attend your nearest out of hours medical centre which will feel as though it is a million miles away – even if it isn't!

Whilst you are waiting for the water to boil, browse through the emergency tip sections in this book. If you ever come face-to-face with an emergency situation you might remember what you should do. Of course, the chances of this happening are very slim, but if one person's life could be saved by someone who has read one of our Sandpiper emergency tips then as a team, our work in putting this book together would be rewarded.

My thanks to BASICS-Scotland and all the Sandpiper GPs, nurses and paramedics who have fed us not only their recipes but their medical guidance/support; to Strutt and Parker and Scottish Rugby Union for their continuing support of the charity and to all those who have sent in recipes.

My final thanks go to my four Aberdeenshire elves; Kate Robertson, Miranda McHardy, Virginia Fyffe and Bev Remp for their invaluable contribution to this cookbook.

Claire Maitland
CO-FOUNDER OF THE SANDPIPER TRUST

Recipe for Life

1 tongue – that does not slander
1 heart – generous and kind
2 ears – closed to gossip
2 eyes – overlooking others faults
1 mind – full of tolerance
2 hands – extended to help others
1 dash of wit, sunny disposition and cheerfulness

Blend together the above ingredients.
Form into one being.
Serve generous portions to everyone you meet daily.

Anon

contents

"

A cold Saturday morning in December. It's early hours, I see the number flashing on my mobile – Ambulance call out.

Two vehicle accident on the A9. I run downstairs, pull on my high-vis suit, turn on the siren and lights on the car and I'm off. Another high-speed collision, two killed instantly, two trapped. It's cold and wet and the extrication is challenging. Casualty conditions keep changing, and so too do our priorities – triage and treat. We work fast, but with care. It's all about team work – paramedic and doctor, police and fire crews. Problems-a-plenty need quick solutions. Think about what you say... and who might hear. Talk to, and constantly reassure frightened casualties. Rotor blades – the helicopter ambulance arrives. The injured finally released... Sandpiper equipment and vehicle locator vital once again.

GP, Aviemore, Inverness-shire

early starts
& quick fixes

Early start
1. Early-morning start to a person's day. Set off early. The earliest calculated date on which an activity can begin.

Quick fix
1. An approach to finding a solution to a problem as quickly as possible. A solution which meets urgent needs. A rapid repair.

Brie & Bacon Butty

PER PERSON

1 crusty roll
3 rashers of streaky bacon
3 slices of brie
Sour cream and chive dip
Tomato ketchup

Grill bacon until crisp. Slice and butter a roll. Lay the sizzling bacon on each half followed by the strips of brie. Toast under the grill until the cheese has melted. Add sour cream and chive dip and ketchup and serve.

Richard Drysdale
KILRIE, FIFE

Crunchy Dry Cereal

USE AS A CEREAL OR SPRINKLE ON FRUIT

275g oats
110g sesame seeds
110g wheatgerm
110g dessicated coconut
9 tablespoons runny honey
3 tablespoons sunflower oil
1 teaspoon vanilla extract (not flavouring)

Combine dry ingredients, gently warm oil, honey and vanilla, add to dry ingredients and combine thoroughly.
    Spread in baking tray and cook slowly, turning often, until golden brown. When it's quite cold, store in an airtight jar.

Sue Clapham
YTHANWELLS, ABERDEENSHIRE

Double Toasted Muesli

1 cup sesame seeds
1 cup sunflower seeds
1 cup whole unblanched almonds
4 cups rolled oats
1 cup wheatgerm
1 cup bran
1 cup sunflower oil
Honey
1 cup water

Toast sesame seeds by shaking in a non-stick frying pan. Crush almonds with a rolling pin to make large crunchy pieces. Toss oats with wheatgerm and bran. Heat oil, water and honey together and mix with the oats. Spread onto a large baking sheet and bake for about 25 minutes. Mix in all the nuts and seeds and bake for a further 5-10 minutes.

Diana Seymour

5-minute Cheese on Toast

SERVES 4

8 slices of baguette
2 tomatoes
4 slices goat's cheese (or other cheese)
Basil leaves
A little olive oil

Toast the bread on one side. Flip the slices over and top with a slice of tomato, cheese and a basil leaf. Drizzle each one with olive oil . Grill until the cheese just melts.

Noelle Fyffe
FETTERNEAR, ABERDEENSHIRE

Tuna Melts

SERVES 2

1 can tuna in brine, drained
3 to 4 pieces of toast
Hellmann's mayonnaise
Slices of cheese, enough to cover toasts

Roughly mash up drained tuna, mix with about 2 tablespoons mayonnaise and spread thickly on toast. Top with slices of cheese (mousetrap for instance) and bung in a hot oven till cheese starting to melt and it is hot right through. *Voila!*

Kirstie Daranyi
DRUMMUIR, BANFFSHIRE

Basil Houmous

1 can chick peas
Olive oil
Salt and pepper
2 cloves garlic
Juice and zest of 1 lemon
Handful basil

Drain the can of chick peas and put in liquidiser. Add a generous dash of olive oil, salt and pepper, about 2 cloves of garlic and the juice of a lemon (and zest if you want). Whizz up and then add a huge handful (about half a supermarket plant) of basil and whizz again. Yummy (better than normal houmous). And lasts well in fridge for days.

Bella Forbes
KEIG, ABERDEENSHIRE

Artichoke Dip

1 can artichoke hearts
1 x 225g tub *Philadelphia* cheese
Half cup mayonnaise
Three quarters cup grated parmesan
Fresh dill
Cayenne pepper

Preheat oven to 190°C, gas mark 5.
Put all ingredients into a food processor and whizz until smooth. Put in ovenproof dish and bake in oven for 2 minutes. Serve with crudités.

Diane Hastings
EDINBURGH

Baked Oatmeal

SERVES 4/6

Half cup vegetable oil (not olive – it's too strong)
2 eggs
1 cup dark brown sugar
3 cups oatmeal (porridge oats)
2 teaspoons baking powder
Half teaspoon salt
1 cup milk

Preheat oven to 180°C, gas mark 4.
Combine all dry ingredients, then add all the wet ones and mix quickly. Pour into a well greased ovenproof dish and bake for about 45 minutes, until it is no longer sticky in the middle. Serve with stewed fruit, yogurt or cold milk.

Janet MacKenzie
DUNBLANE, PERTHSHIRE

Hill Runner's Porridge

PER PERSON

Half cup porridge oats
1 and half cups water
Handful stoned prunes
2 bananas
2 teaspoons Manuka honey

Microwave 4 minutes, or stir in a saucepan until cooked through. Add prunes, bananas or honey (or all three on race days...)

Dr Neil Arnott
FORT WILLIAM, HIGHLANDS

Jess's Sunday Night Supper

PER PERSON

2 eggs
Butter
Ham
Cheese
Cream (optional)

Take a small ramekin dish and butter liberally. Chop up some ham, or pieces of chopped cooked bacon, and place in bottom of dish. Break the eggs on top add a little cheese and a couple of tablespoons of cream (if you don't use cream add extra butter), and a knob of butter. Season to taste with salt and pepper.

Put in a hot oven for 10 minutes until the cheese is melted. Serve with Marmite soldiers.

Jessica Dickson
DOUNE, PERTHSHIRE

TIP... The rooster may crow... but the hen delivers the goods!

Woodend Olives

ANYTIME SNACK

Kalamata olives
Garlic cloves
Fresh thyme
5 black peppercorns
Lemon zest
Olive oil
Coriander seed

Pound up all herbs and olive oil. Add drained olives. Eat when you like.

Miranda McHardy
BANCHORY, KINCARDINESHIRE

Kettle Poached Eggs

Eggs
Cling film
Glass

Put clingfilm loosely over the glass. Break an egg into the clingfilm. Fold up the sides of the clingfilm and twist together so as little air is in the parcel as possible

Fill a kettle or a pan full of water put the eggs in and bring to the boil. Boil to taste.

Drop the parcel into cold water and unwrap.

John Drysdale
KILRIE, FIFE

The Sandpiper Sandwich

PER PERSON

2 slices brown bread
1 envelope – brown
110g cheese
50g ham
1 teaspoon mayonnaise
1 x £20 note
1 teaspoon mustard

Lightly butter bread. Chop the ham and grate cheese. Fold into mayonnaise and mustard. Spread on bread and sandwich together. Fold £20 note and put into a brown envelope and whisk off to The Sandpiper Trust (see address on inside back cover). Eat sandwich with relish knowing that you have helped a very good cause.

Knockout Figs – Guaranteed Knockout!

SERVES 2/4

For breakfast, lunch or supper
6 fresh ripe figs
450g smoky bacon – preferably streaky
1 dessertspoonful of maple syrup

Fry all the bacon until crisp – leave the fat in the pan. Cut the figs into quarters (top to bottom) and sauté until soft: add the maple syrup and serve. If this isn't knockout try vodka shots instead. From one for whom it always works!

The Broich
DOUNE, PERTHSHIRE

Cheesey Nibbles

60g butter
110g plain flour
25g rice krispies
110g grated cheese
Cayenne pepper to taste

Preheat oven to 185°C, gas mark 6. Combine the butter and flour to crumbly texture. Add all other ingredients and mix. Add water if necessary. Roll GENTLY into a sausage. Cut into slices and put onto a tray. Cook for 10 minutes or until brownish.

Judy Shaw-Stewart
DOUNE, PERTHSHIRE

Quick Thin Pizza

1 wrap topped with
5/6 tablespoons of tomato purée
Handful of grated cheddar cheese
Sprinkling of thin ham
Put In a hot oven for 2-4 minutes

Ed Clerk
PENICUIK, MIDLOTHIAN

Pearson's Piece

A superior sandwich filling
Mash steamed salmon or sea trout with a small amount of mayonnaise & Japanese soy sauce (Kikoman) until you get a satisfactory consistency for a sandwich filling. A little black pepper can also be added to taste.

Charles Pearson
DUNECHT, ABERDEENSHIRE

Rosemary Nuts

350g mixed salt free nuts – pecan, cashew walnut, hazelnuts
3 sprigs rosemary
2 teaspoons brown sugar
1 teaspoon salt
Half teaspoon cayenne pepper
1 tablespoon melted unsalted butter.

Chop rosemary. Heat the nuts until golden. Mix all the other ingredients and then add hot nuts. Very delicious and very fattening I imagine.

Alexandra Etherington
ZEALS, WILTSHIRE

Roquefort Biscuits

110g self-raising flour
110g butter
50g Roquefort cheese or Stilton – anything blue – grated
50g strong cheddar – grated
50g sesame seeds – toasted

Preheat oven to 180°C, gas mark 6.
Rub the butter and flour together until it resembles fine breadcrumbs, add the cheese and form into a dough. Form small (2cm) balls and roll each one in sesame seeds to coat and press lightly with fork to flatten out slightly. Put onto covered baking sheet or a non-stick one and bake in the oven for 10 minutes until golden.

Keep in an airtight container. And try not to eat them all at once.

Mary McGowan
PONTELAND, NORTHUMBERLAND

Scrambled Eggs with Smoked Salmon

Transform a simple every-day dish into a luxurious supper or Sunday brunch for one. Double the quantities for two persons.

2 large eggs
50g smoked salmon trimmings – readily available from most supermarkets
2 tablespoons of milk
25g butter
Freshly ground salt and pepper

Chop the smoked salmon into smallish pieces. Put the pieces into a cup or a small bowl and pour the milk over them. Leave on one side for about 20 minutes. Break the eggs into a bowl and beat them well with the salt and pepper.

Then, over a gentle heat, melt 10g of the butter in a small heavy saucepan until it is foaming and swirl around the sides of the pan. Add the eggs and stir continuously with a wooden spoon until they begin to solidify. When you have a mixture which is half solid and half liquid, add the smoked salmon pieces, (which by now should have absorbed all the milk). When almost all the liquid has gone, remove from the heat, add the remaining 10g of butter and continue stirring. Serve immediately with triangles of fried bread, or buttered wholemeal toast or sesame toast.

Sheila Rhind
CRATHES, KINCARDINESHIRE

Summer Porridge

SERVES LOTS OF PEOPLE!

6 handfuls of porridge oats
1 handful chopped dates
1 handful flaked almonds
1 handful chopped walnuts
1 handful bran – optional
Blueberries
Strawberries or raspberries
Milk
Natural yoghurt – optional
Apples

Mix porridge oats, dates, almonds walnuts and bran together and put into an airtight container to keep.

The evening before you want some summer porridge for breakfast put one handful of the 'porridge' into a bowl, cover with milk and put it in the fridge overnight. Before breakfast, grate an apple into it, skin and all, (2 handfuls, 2 apples) then add some strawberries or raspberries and blueberries. One handful with the apple and fruit made up will feed two or three people for breakfast depending on your appetite.

Eat with natural yogurt or not as you like. If you don't finish it up, it will keep in the fridge for a couple of days. The dried mixture keeps for weeks in the store cupboard so make plenty then you always have it to hand.

Miranda McHardy
BANCHORY, KINCARDINESHIRE

Sunblush Tomatoes

These are expensive to buy and so easy to make yourself.

Plum tomatoes are best but any will do,
if you have a glut.
Garlic cloves just cracked open not crushed
Black peppercorns
Coriander seeds
Bay leaf
Dried herbs
Olive oil

Preheat oven to 140°C, gas mark 1. Cover a baking sheet with baking parchment, lay the halved tomatoes out onto it. Put the tomatoes into a very cool oven, top left aga – an airing cupboard would probably do! Or a Belling hot cupboard. You do not want to cook them, just dry them out. Leave for about 8-12 hours, keep an eye on them, they should be not completely dried.

Put them all into a jar with a good fitting lid – a Kilner would be ideal – with the garlic and herbs. Cover with good olive oil. They will keep for ages. Marinate for a few days before you eat them. Add to salads, or a plate of salami and shaved Parmesan for a great 5 second starter.

Miranda McHardy
BANCHORY, KINCARDINESHIRE

Homemade Houmous

400g tin chickpeas
2 cloves garlic – chopped up very small
1 dessertspoon tahini – sesame seed paste available from supermarkets and health food shops
Sea salt to taste
1 teaspoon cumin powder
Approximately 100-200ml water
1 teaspoon lemon juice (optional)

Put all the ingredients into blender. Then add 100ml water. Continue adding water bit by bit to allow the mixture to blend effectively. The finished consistency should be thick – not runny. Enjoy with vegetable crudités or pitta bread / salad.

Alison Hay
INVERURIE CHARTERED PHYSIOTHERAPY CLINIC

Prince Youssoupoff's Russian eggs

6 eggs
2 teaspoonful Dijon mustard
Dash of double cream
Freshly chopped chives
Freshly ground salt and white pepper

Boil the eggs and cut them in half
Take the yolks out and mash them with the mustard, salt and pepper, cream and chives
Mix well and fill into the white halves.
Serve on a silver platter with some unsalted buttered toast.

Philip Astor
TILLYPRONIE, ABERDEENSHIRE

Smoked Mackerel Paté and Melba Toast

6 fillets smoked mackerel – peppered
110g full fat soft cream cheese
1 large tablespoon horseradish
Juice of 1 lemon
150ml double cream
Pinch of salt and pepper

Skin the mackeral fillets and blend together with all the other ingredients.

Melba Toast
Toast some white bread then cut off the crusts. Now carefully slice between the toast to make two thin pieces out of one. Re-toast each piece until crisp – do not burn.

Seve the paté with the warm toast, lemon wedges and fresh green salad leaves

Bob Ovington
PITTODRIE HOUSE HOTEL

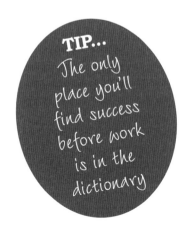

TIP...
The only place you'll find success before work is in the dictionary

THE
BIG
PUSH

after Ben Shahn, 1957

Our staff constantly travel the length and breadth of Scotland and work in precisely those remote and rural areas covered by the GPs that are being equipped by Sandpiper. Many of our clients own properties and employ gamekeepers, foresters, farm workers and estate tradesmen who work in those remote and rural areas.

We are all at risk of an accident in those areas and the fact that such a life might be saved as a result of the emergency equipment provided by Sandpiper explains exactly why the charity is so important and relevant to us as a business.

From our point of view, Strutt and Parker value the support Sandpiper provides to rural doctors in the areas in which we work, and we wish it continued success in the future

Strutt and Parker – Property Consultants
Banchory
Edinburgh
Glasgow
Inverness

soups & starters

Soup *n.* **1**. a liquid food made by boiling or simmering meat, fish, vegetables etc., usually served hot at the beginning of a meal. **2**. *Informal.* a photographic developer. **3**. *Informal.* anything resembling soup in appearance or consistency, esp. thick fog. **4. in the soup.** *Informal.* in trouble or difficulties.

Starter *n.* **1**. Also called: **self-starter.** a device for starting an internal-combustion engine, usually consisting of a powerful electric motor that engages with a flywheel. **2**. a person who supervises and signals the start of a race. **3**. *Chiefly Brit.* the first course of a meal. **4. for starters.** *Slang.* in the first place.

Gazpacho, served with Olive Bread

SERVES 6 AS A STARTER

900g ripe tomatoes – chopped
Half cucumber – peeled and chopped
1 small green pepper – deseeded and chopped
1 small red pepper – deseeded and chopped
1 red onion – chopped
2 cloves garlic – crushed
2 tablespoons extra virgin olive oil
2 tablespoons of red wine vinegar
1 tablespoon parsley – chopped
Pinch of sugar
Sea salt and freshly ground black pepper
600ml tomato juice
180ml ice cold water

Croutons
2 slices white bread – cubed
Sunflower oil – for frying

Garnish
Finely diced red and green pepper, red onion, cucumber
2 tablespoons chopped parsley

Olive bread to serve
I loaf Pan Gallego or Ciabatta bread
100g unsalted butter
6 black olives – stoned and finely chopped
6 green olives – stoned and finely chopped
Freshly ground black pepper

Preparation time: 35 minutes, plus chilling.
Cooking time: 20-25 minutes. Oven: 200° C, gas mark 6

Liquidise the first 11 ingredients until smooth. Add the tomato juice and process again. Pour into a large bowl and stir in the water. Adjust the seasoning and add more water if necessary. Chill well before serving.

Slice the bread at 12mm intervals, cutting the loaf almost all the way through but keeping the base intact.

Soften the butter and stir in the chopped olives and ground black pepper. Spread the olive butter between the slices of bread. Wrap the bread in foil and bake for 20-25 minutes, until the butter has melted and the bread is hot.

Heat the sunflower oil in a small pan and fry the white bread cubes for a couple of minutes until crisp. Drain the croutons on kitchen paper.

Serve the warm olive bread with the chilled soup, garnished with the above vegetables, parsley and croutons.

Philippa Nagel
DURRIS, KINCARDINESHIRE

TIP...
If you leave the root end — the hairy one — on your onion whilst slicing it, you won't cry

Pea Soup

SERVES 6/8 HOT OR COLD

75g butter
1 onion
1-2 cloves garlic – cut finely
Large handful mint – chopped
450g frozen peas
1.2 litre chicken stock
150ml single cream
Juice of half a lemon

Melt butter. Add onion , garlic and mint and soften. Add frozen peas and chicken stock. Cook for 10-15 minutes. Liquidise.
HOT: Add cream and lemon juice and serve
COLD: Cool and leave in fridge for two hours or more then add the cream and lemon juice just before serving.

Mo Farquharson
WHITEHOUSE, ABERDEENSHIRE

Cold Summer Soup

SERVES 4

12 fresh, trimmed mint leaves
2 tins consommé
450ml tomato juice
225ml sour cream

Blend the trimmed mint leaves with one can of consommé. Add the rest of the ingredients with a teaspoon of sugar. Blend and refrigerate overnight.
Place crossed pieces of mint on soup in each bowl to serve.

Pat Norris
MONTREAL, CANADA

Red Pepper and Tomato Soup

SERVES 8

Olive oil
1 onion – chopped
3 large red peppers – seeded and chopped
2 cans of chopped tomatoes
Half litre vegetable stock
60ml dry sherry
280ml single cream
Salt and pepper

Fry onion and pepper in oil in large pan for 5 minutes, add tomatoes and stock and simmer for 25 minutes. Purée and return to the pan. Add the cream, reheat gently, add sherry and salt and pepper to taste.

Barbara Manson
OLDMELDRUM, ABERDEENSHIRE

Sweet Potato, Chilli and Coconut Soup

SERVES 4/6

2 large leeks, sliced or one large red onion chopped
4 large sweet potatoes – cubed
1 tablespoonful of olive oil
Small piece of fresh ginger – chopped
2 cloves of garlic – chopped
1 parsnip, cubed (optional)
Vegetable stock (to cover about 1 litre)
Coconut milk – half a tin
Lime juice
Chilli to taste
Salt and pepper
Fresh coriander leaves for the garnish

Sweet Potato, Chilli and Coconut Soup continued...

Sweat the leeks or onions in olive oil with the ginger, garlic and chilli. Add the sweet potatoes and cook for a few minutes before adding the stock. Simmer until the vegetables are tender. Blend soup together with the coconut milk and reheat (gently or the milk will split). Add lime juice to taste and season with salt and pepper. Garnish with freshly chopped coriander.

Alternative garnishes: Crumbled prawn crackers; toasted coconut or freshly grated coconut; fried chorizo slices.

Gillian Vieilledent
LUMPHANAN, ABERDEENSHIRE

Very Simple Soup

SERVES 4/6

2 onions – chopped
2 cloves garlic – chopped
4-5 courgettes – chopped
Olive oil
1.2 litres chicken stock
Bunch of herbs – mint or rosemary
Chives to finish

Fry off the onions and garlic. Add the courgettes. Cook until soft. Pour in the stock and add the add the herbs. Simmer for 20 minutes. Liquidise and serve with crème fraiche or natural yoghurt and chives

Meg White
ABOYNE, ABERDEENSHIRE

Roasted Butternut Squash Soup with Parmesan Croutons

SERVES 4/6

Large butternut squash – peeled and cubed
One large onion – chopped
2 tablespoonfuls of olive oil
1 or 2 sprigs of fresh thyme
2 cloves garlic – chopped
1 dessertspoon mild curry powder
Vegetable stock (about 1 to 2 litres)
Salt and pepper
Double cream – optional

Spread the squash out on a baking tray and sprinkle with some of the olive oil. Season with salt, pepper and thyme. Roast in a hot oven until slightly blackened at the edges – around 25 minutes.

Fry the onion and garlic in a saucepan until soft and translucent. Add the curry powder and then scrape the squash and all juices and thyme from the baking tray into the pan. Add the stock and simmer for 5 minutes. Blend the soup and season to taste. Add some double cream before serving and top with a few parmesan croutons.

Parmesan Croutons
Cube a ready-to-bake baguette and put in a bowl. Add some olive oil and grate over lots of Parmesan cheese. Stir well to coat. Season with rock salt and pepper and spread out on a baking tray. Put in oven at 200°C for about 7 minutes, checking so they don't burn. It's also very good if crumbled thyme leaves are added with the cheese.

Gillian Vieilledent,
LUMPHANAN, ABERDEENSHIRE

Crème Taj Mahal

SERVES 4/6

25g butter
Half tablespoon mild curry powder
225g dessert apples, peeled and chopped
125g onion chopped
225g canned tomatoes
25g flour
850ml water
1 and half chicken stock cubes
2 tablespoons lemon juice
65ml fresh single cream
Salt and pepper

Melt butter in a saucepan, add curry powder, apple and onion. Gently cook till onion is soft but not coloured. Blend in flour and cook for one minute. Stir in canned tomatoes with juice, water and stock cubes. Simmer for ten minutes, then add lemon juice. Cool. Liquidise. Add salt and pepper and add half the cream. Chill the soup until required and then stir in the remainder of the cream and serve. This soup can also be served hot.

Alice Wallace
STRATHDON, ABERDEENSHIRE

Scotch Broth

SERVES 4

1.5 litres of chicken stock
1 small turnip – chopped
I large carrot – chopped
1 leek – chopped
1 onion – chopped
25g broth mix
Chopped parsley

Put broth mix in pan of chicken stock. Bring to boil, cover and simmer for half an hour. Add chopped vegetables. Simmer for an hour. Add leeks. Cook for a final half hour. Season with salt and pepper. Before serving add chopped parsley.

Inchmarlo Golf Centre
BANCHORY, KINCARDINESHIRE

Root Soup

SERVES 6

2 large parsnips – peeled and chopped
1 small sweet potato – peeled and chopped
Half a small turnip – peeled and chopped
1 onion – peeled and chopped
1 leek – washed and chopped
3 large carrots – chopped
1 dessertspoon olive oil
Approx 1 litre water
Sea salt and pepper to taste

Soften onion in olive oil for 5 minutes. Add all other vegetables and allow to sweat for 5 minutes. Add 1 litre water (you can add more, depending how thick you want your soup) and seasoning. Simmer for 30 minutes. Blend, serve and enjoy!

Alison Hay
INVERURIE CHARTERED PHYSIOTHERAPY CLINIC

TIP...
If no time to do the ironing, put it in the deep freeze until you are ready to do it

Farmhouse Mushroom Soup

SERVES 4/6

40g unsalted butter or margarine
2 medium onions – chopped
230g mushrooms – wiped and chopped
(use well-flavoured, large mushrooms
to give maximum taste to the soup)
2 tablespoons flour
1.2 litres good quality chicken
or vegetable stock
1 tablespoon long grained rice
1 bay leaf
Salt and freshly ground black pepper

Melt the butter in a large pan. Stir in onions
and cook for 5 minutes to soften. Add
mushrooms and continue to cook for a
further 3 minutes. Stir in the flour, then
gradually add stock stirring all the time.
Bring slowly to the boil, stir in rice and bay
leaf. Simmer for 15-20 minutes. Remove the
bay leaf. Process in liquidiser or food
processor to required texture. Return soup
to pan. Reheat, then taste and add
seasoning as required. Serve piping hot
with a dash of cream if wished.

Mary Haggard
BLEATHWOOD, SHROPSHIRE

Easy Yummy Butternut Soup

SERVES 6

Nutritious and recommended for people
who suffer from chronic fatigue!

Half a medium sized Butternut squash
4 carrots
1 onion
3 sweet potatoes
1 stick of celery
3 medium potatoes
1.5 litres chicken stock
Olive oil

Chop up everything fairly roughly. Put
chopped onion into saucepan, and fry gently
in olive oil, turning all the time so it doesn't
burn, until soft. Then add all vegetables on a
fairly high heat and turn them over and over
to get them covered in oil and allow them to
sweat a bit. Add the chicken stock and some
water if necessary to cover everything well.

Cook slowly for approx 1 hour, until all the
vegetables are tender. Mash it with a potato
masher, or whiz it in a food processor until it
is the consistency you like. If you want to be
posh serve it with chopped coriander and a
tiny swirl of olive oil. To make it really tasty
you can sprinkle with a little parmesan.

Emma Pattullo
PLATFORM 22, TORPHINS, ABERDEENSHIRE

French Onion Soup

SERVES 6

700g onions – sliced
2 cloves garlic – crushed
50g butter
2 tablespoons oil
Half teaspoon granulated sugar
1.2 litres good beef stock
275ml dry white wine
Salt and pepper
1-2 tablespoons brandy
1 baguette
Emmenthal, Gruyére or Jarlsberg cheese

In large saucepan, heat the butter and oil together. Add the onions, garlic and sugar and cook over a low heat, stir occasionally for about 30 minutes or until caramelised. Add the stock and wine, bring to boil and simmer with lid on for about one hour. Season and add brandy if wished.
   Serve with lightly toasted thick slices of baguette smothered with grated cheese of choice, place under grill until it is bubbly and golden.

Gordon Riley
PARAMEDIC – BANCHORY, KINCARDINESHIRE

TIP...
The greatest pleasure in life is achieving what people tell you is unachievable

The Hapsburg Pheasant Broth

SERVES 6

Bouillon ingredients
2 pheasants, old or young, fresh or frozen. Defrost if necessary, skin them, cut off breasts and legs and lay them aside.
6 potatoes – peeled and cut in quarters
6 carrots –peeled and sliced
3 leeks – the white part
4 garlic cloves
2 shallots
8 black peppercorns
7 juniper berries
4 bay leaves
Half a Savoy cabbage
4 slices Black Forest ham (or smoked bacon)

Soup ingredients
The pheasant breasts and legs (see above)
7 potatoes – freshly peeled and quartered
7 carrots – freshly peeled and sliced
2 tablespoons fresh soured cream
1 large glass dry white wine

Use a big pot, fill three quarters with water. Dissolve two chicken stock cubes, put in the pheasant carcasses, and rest of the ingredients. Bring to the boil and let simmer for one & half hours. Strain and put bouillon back into the pot. Add the pheasant breasts and legs, preferably boned, the potatoes and carrots. Let simmer until ingredients are cooked. Before adding fresh sour cream, pour the wine into the broth and stir. Serve hot in a warmed soup tureen.

Philip Astor WITH ASSISTANCE FROM
MONICA VON HOUSEKEEPER
TILLYPRONIE, ABERDEENSHIRE

Courgette Soup

SERVES 4

1 tablespoon olive oil
1 onion chopped
4 medium courgettes sliced
1 litre chicken stock
Freshly ground salt and pepper

Heat the oil in a medium sized pan and add the onion. Cook for 2-3 minutes until softened but not browned. Add the courgettes and cook for 2 minutes.
   Add the chicken stock and bring to the boil; then simmer for 20 minutes.
   Allow to cool slightly and then blend until smooth. Return to the saucepan and adjust the seasoning, reheat gently and then serve immediately in 4 warm serving bowls.

Gordon Ramsay
THE F WORD

Karelian Fish Soup

SERVES 2/4

1 fillet each of various fish – cut into strips of 3-5cm (ideally coarse river or lake fish, eg perch, pike, eel, but as these are not easily available; sea fish will do
– eg cod, haddock, halibut, salmon)
1 medium potato – cubed into fine cubes
1 large carrot – cubed into fine cubes
1 medium onion – chopped
1 bunch of parsley –finely chopped
1 bunch of dill – finely chopped
1 bunch of chives – finely chopped
1 knob of butter
2 tablespoons of vegetable oil

1 litre of fish stock (ideally prepared from fish bones and heads; stock cube will do)
Freshly ground salt and pepper

Glaze onion in butter and oil, add potato and carrot cubes, add fish stock and let simmer for some 10-15 minutes or until carrot is tender. Add fish and let simmer for not more than 5 minutes. Season with salt and pepper and add parsley, dill and chives. Serve immediately.

Dr Peter Raff
DRUMMORE, STRANRAER

Neep Bree

SERVES 6

A famous Scots Chef once asked me: "What can you possibly do with a turnip?"
   He was mocking Scots vegetables at the time, suggesting they were not good enough to use in his restaurant and that there was no alternative but to import everything from France. This is one of my favourite ways of using a turnip! It is a delicious soup and has always been a huge favourite of my customers. Bree is an old Scots word for "broth"

1 large neep (a yellow swede turnip to uninitiated) – peeled and diced small. Should weigh approximately 500g when prepared – discard woody parts.
2 onions – peeled and chopped small
Finely grated rind and juice of 1 large orange
Piece of whole root ginger, approximately size of top of thumb – finely grated

50g butter
1 litre vegetable stock
125ml milk approximately plus
125ml double cream to serve
Salt and pepper
Freshly chopped chives

Melt butter in large saucepan until foaming Add onions. Turn in butter until soft, but not brown. Add turnip and stir together well with onion. Add grated ginger, plus sprinkle of salt and pepper. Put lid on and allow vegetables to cook gently for 5-10 minutes, stirring occasionally. Pour in orange juice and rind and stir well. Add stock and bring to the boil, then reduce heat and simmer with lid on for 1 hour. Add milk and liquidise thoroughly (it could be cooled and frozen at this stage).

Check seasoning to taste and stir cream through. Heat thoroughly before serving, and sprinkle finely chopped chives. If too thick, add a little more milk or cream.

Shirley Spear
THE THREE CHIMNEYS RESTAURANT, ISLE OF SKYE

Spicy Lentil Soup

SERVES 6

400g red split lentils
Half teaspoon turmeric
Half teaspoon chilli
Half teaspoon coriander powder
1 teaspoon cumin
2/3 litres chicken stock
1 small onion – chopped
2 cloves garlic
Olive oil

Sweat the onion and garlic in olive oil until soft, and add cumin, chilli, turmeric, and coriander. Add red lentils, salt and pepper and stir together for a couple of minutes. Add chicken stock and simmer slowly for a couple of hours stirring occasionally.

David Ogilvy
CORTACHY, ANGUS

Sweet Potato Soup

SERVES 4/6

1 onion – chopped
1 clove garlic – crushed
3 carrots – chopped
2 sweet potatoes – chopped
125g red lentils – washed
1 litre chicken or vegetable stock
400g tin tomatoes
1 teaspoon paprika
1 teaspoon mixed herbs
1 teaspoon olive oil

Soften onion in oil over a medium heat, add vegetables and garlic and cook for five minutes. Add well rinsed lentils with spices and stir until well combined. Add tomatoes and stock, bring to boil and simmer for 20 minutes or until vegetables are cooked. Liquidise and season to taste

Dr Mark and Mrs Kirsty Simpson
MID ARGYLL COMMUNITY HOSPITAL, LOCHGILPHEAD

Watercress Soup

SERVES 4

2 bunches of watercress
3 large leeks
2 medium potatoes – peeled and chopped
50g butter
845ml chicken stock
150ml double cream
Freshly ground salt and pepper

Chop white parts of leeks and take stalks off watercress. Melt butter, add leeks, potatoes and watercress. Add salt, cover and sweat over a low heat for about 20 minutes, stirring from time-to-time. Add stock and simmer, covered for 15 more minutes. Add cream and serve hot or cold.

Gilly Snelling
COUPAR ANGUS, PERTHSHIRE

Creamed Country Vegetable Soup

SERVES 6

1 medium onion
1 medium potato
1 medium carrot
1 small piece of swede (turnip)
50g butter
570ml stock (made with vegetable or chicken stock cube)
150ml milk (approx)
Freshly ground salt and pepper

Peel and slice all the vegetables. Place the butter in the saucepan and allow to melt.

Add the vegetables and fry gently for about 5 minutes. Add the stock and bring to the boil and allow to simmer until all vegetables are soft – about 20 minutes. Taste and add salt and pepper if required. Liquidise until smooth and add enough milk to give the consistency of thin cream. Re-heat before serving.

Carina McGuinness
EAST LINTON, EAST LOTHIAN

Goulash Soup

SERVES 6

500g lean stewing steak – diced in 1cm cubes
1 tablespoon plain flour
Freshly ground salt and pepper
2 tablespoons olive oil
4 tomatoes peeled – cored and diced
1 tablespoon tomato purée
2 heaped teaspoons paprika
1 large onion – chopped
1 medium sized carrot – grated
1 clove garlic – crushed or chopped
Quarter teaspoon cayenne pepper
One and a half teaspoons paprika powder
2 bay leaves
Herbs – thyme, rosemary, parsley
750ml water

OPTIONAL
Quarter teaspoon cumin powder
Quarter teaspoon ground caraway seed
More vegetables eg peas, green beans
– chopped
To add more substance you could add carbohydrates eg potato, rice or pasta.

Add these at the end of the cooking process allowing 25 minutes

Rub flour, salt and pepper into the cubed beef. Shake off any surplus flour. Heat a heavy saucepan with the olive oil and sear the meat for about 3 minutes.

Add the chopped onions, peppers and carrot and also any fresh herbs you might be using. Any surplus flour should also be added at this stage. Stir for 5 minutes on a medium heat. Dissolve all the debris that might become stuck to the bottom of your pot. Add 750ml of water and all the other ingredients. Bring to the boil and simmer for 2 hours (lid on pan, stirring occasionally).

You may have to add extra water, especially if adding carbohydrates.

Dr Rachel Weldon
ISLE OF EIGG

Tortellini Soup
A Sunday Night Special

SERVES 6

400g tin consommé
400g tin chopped tomatoes
225g tortellini (any flavour)
110g mushrooms – sliced
110g spinach – cleaned, stemmed and torn
50g Parmesan cheese
6 fresh basil leaves
3/4 cloves garlic
1 teaspoon butter

Sauté finely chopped garlic in butter. Add consommé and bring to boil. Add tortellini

and simmer for about 6/8 minutes. Add tomatoes, spinach, mushrooms and basil. Simmer for 2/3 minutes. Stir in grated Parmesan and serve.

Claire Maitland
CRATHES, KINCARDINESHIRE

Wonder Plant Soup

SERVES 4

Silky smooth and highly nutritious, this watercress soup provides loads of B vitamins, great carotene and iron and powerful anti-oxidants. 10 minutes preparation time, 20 minutes cooking time.

1 onion – chopped
2 big bunches washed watercress and some for garnish
1 medium potato – diced
1 tablespoon sunflower oil
1 litre real vegetable stock
125ml natural yoghurt
Freshly ground salt and pepper

In a good sized pan, lightly cook onion, watercress and potato in the oil for about 5 minutes. Add the stock, simmer for 10 minutes, liquidise till smooth. Season with little salt. Put soup back in pan, heat thoroughly, serve and add a spoonful of yoghurt. Garnish with the Wonder Plant.

Laurie Mill
METHVEN, PERTHSHIRE

Peterkin's Pea Soup

SERVES 6

55g butter
4 green onions – chopped
455g fresh or frozen green peas
590ml vegetable broth or stock
3 tablespoons chopped fresh mint leaves
590ml milk
Freshly ground salt and pepper
Pinch white sugar (optional)
4 tablespoons light whipping cream
2 sprigs fresh mint leaves for garnish

Melt butter in a large saucepan over a low heat. Add the onions, and cook until softened, but not brown. Stir in the peas, vegetable stock and mint. Increase heat to medium and bring to a boil. Reduce heat back to low, cover, and let simmer for about 30 minutes. If you are using frozen peas, 15 minutes is enough. Using a large slotted spoon, remove about 3 tablespoons of the peas, and set aside for garnish. Put the soup into a blender or food processor along with the milk, and puree until smooth. Season to taste. Add pinch of sugar if desired. Allow the soup to cool to room temperature then refrigerate until chilled.

Pour soup into 4 serving bowls. Swirl 1 tablespoon of light cream into each one, then garnish with the reserved peas and springs of mint. 'It's easy my wife tells me – and I find it tasty.'

Professor Gordon Peterkin
THE SCOTTISH CENTRE FOR TELEHEALTH
FORESTERHILL, ABERDEEN

Lettuce Soup

SERVES 4

2 lettuces
50g butter
50g flour
Whipping cream
Half chicken stock cube
1.2 litres milk
Chopped chives
Drop of vinegar
Freshly ground salt and pepper

Chop lettuce very finely. Put in saucepan with butter. Add flour, chives, stock cube and milk and stir until thickens. Add a drop of vinegar and serve hot or cold with a swirl of cream and chopped chives.

Biddy Wood
LAMBERHURST, KENT

TIP...
Before you judge a man, walk a mile in his shoes, after that, who cares, you will be a mile away and you have got his shoes

Potato Soup

SERVES 4

4 spring onions – chopped including all the green
Half a small stick of celery – chopped including leaves
3 medium cooked potatoes or about 6 small cooked new potatoes
1 chicken stock cube or 3 or 4 teaspoons bouillon
800ml boiling water
1 tablespoon vegetable oil
8/10 mint leaves – roughly chopped
Good grinding of pepper

Put oil, spring onions and celery in a saucepan and sweat on a low heat with lid on for a few minutes to soften. Add the potatoes roughly chopped along with the boiling water, bouillon and pepper. Simmer for a few minutes. Add the chopped mint and liquidise with a hand-held whizzer. Put back on stove to heat thoroughly and serve. If you have no mint, use parsley or both.

Anne Pelham Burn
DESS, ABERDEENSHIRE

Spring Green Vitality Soup

SERVES 4

This recipe will work for whichever vegetables you have. Just use a similar quantity – eg half a cauliflower or 2 leeks or 3 courgettes or 2 handfuls of raw spinach/swiss chard or a head of lettuce, frozen peas, nettles!

2 onions (preferably red) – chopped
One third cucumber – unpeeled if organic
1 avocado
Handful fresh coriander or mint
1 tin coconut milk
Handful of leaves or one head of broccoli – whatever Is fresh and in season
1 teaspoon marigold stock powder
Optional – handful of bean sprouts

Gently fry the onions in a little olive or coconut oil until pale and soft. Add any tougher, outer leaves or stalks of broccoli to the onions. Steam your vegetables for 2 or 3 minutes only. Put everything in the liquidiser, whizz until smooth adding a little water keeping it nice and thick. Reheat until warm. Serve with fresh herbs and eat immediately

Jane Lorimer
LEVEN, FIFE

Cucumber Vichyssoise

SERVES 4

1 cucumber – seeded and chopped
450g new potatoes – peeled and sliced
1 onion – chopped
50g butter
1.2 litres chicken stock

Soften the onions in butter over low heat. Add the cucumber and potatoes. Cook with the lid on for 5/10 minutes. Add chicken stock. Simmer for 20 minutes. Liquidise with a little dill if available. Serve hot or cold

Alexandra Stancioff
DUNLUGAS, ABERDEENSHIRE

P's big pot of soup

To make the stock
Skinned pheasant and
a piece of boiling beef
1 or 2 sticks celery, onion, carrot, bayleaf,
peppercorns and water to cover.

Put all in pot and bring to the boil and
simmer for a few hours. Strain liquid into
bowl (not down the sink...). Chop up a bit of
pheasant if it is not too dry and chop up the
meat from the boiling beef and put on one
side. You could of course just use 2 or 3
chicken or vegetable stock cubes.

Now make the soup

1.2 litres of your stock - see above
Olive oil or vegetable oil
2 onions
2 carrots
4 sticks celery
1 sweet potato
1 or 2 leeks
1 potato
1 beef stock cube
Tomato puree
Marmite
Freshly ground salt and pepper
6 heaped tablespoons mixed vegetable
broth dry mix or similar

Chop up all vegetables quite small, either in
a blender or by hand. Heat up few
tablespoons of oil and add all vegetables
and broth – mix and stir around. It will steam
quite a bit. Keep stirring to stop vegetables
sticking. When they have begun to get
soggy, pour in the stock or water and stock
cube. Bring this to the boil and then simmer
slowly for 45 minutes. Taste, start adding

salt, pepper, tomato puree and *Marmite*.
Now you are ready to add the pheasant
and beef bits. Sometimes I cook sausages
and add them chopped. It sounds disgusting
but everyone always eats the sausage bits.
You now have lunch for a week. Make
sure you store it in the fridge. When reheating, always make sure to bring it up to
boiling point.

Penny Dickson
DOUNE, PERTHSHIRE

A Cold Soup

1 melon
Basil
1 lime
Sugar water (3 parts sugar to 1 part water –
heat and dissolve)

Cut and de-seed melon. Scoop out contents
and put in blender with juice of lime plus
several basil leaves. Add sugar water to
taste (if not already sweet enough). Add 1 or
2 intact basil leaves plus 2 to 3 scoops of
melon. Delicious on a warm summer's day.

Dr Noelle Murphy
A & E DEPARTMENT, RAIGMORE, INVERNESS

Smoked Salmon Pâté

SERVES 4

255g smoked salmon
110g cream cheese
2 tablespoons double cream
Half a lemon, juice only
2 tablespoon chopped chives (plus some extra chives to sprinkle over the top)
Pinch of sugar
Freshly ground pepper

Put all ingredients in blender and pulse to desired consistency. [Rough for starter with salad & oatcakes, smooth for canapés]. Add plenty of pepper but no salt, as smoked salmon is salty. Sprinkle chopped chives on top. For a change, substitute the lemon and chives with lime & coriander.

Val Rahtz
ECHT, ABERDEENSHIRE

Twice Baked Goat's Cheese Soufflé

MAKES 8 SOUFFLES IN 275ML MOULD

75g butter
75g self raising flour
570ml milk
350g goat's cheese
7 eggs – separated
Freshly ground salt and pepper
570ml double cream
Parmesan cheese

Preheat oven to 200°C, gas mark 6. Melt the butter, add the flour and heated milk. Stir over a medium heat with balloon whisk to make a white sauce. Stir in the cheese and melt, add salt and pepper. Stir the egg yolks into the sauce. Whisk egg whites until firm and fold carefully into the sauce. Pour into buttered metal moulds and cook in a bain marie (roasting tin with water reaching 1/3 of a way up moulds) for 25 minutes or when risen and golden on top.

Remove from the oven and leave to rest for 10 minutes. Remove soufflés from the moulds using a palette knife and place face down in individual ovenproof dishes or one large ovenproof dish.

Pour cream around the bottom of the soufflés and sprinkle copiously with Parmesan cheese . Return to the oven for ten minutes until risen and golden. Serve immediately on warmed plates. Can be made in advance and kept in the fridge after first stage of cooking.

Mary Anne Rankin
LOCHNAGAR RESTAURANT – KILMALCOLM, AYRSHIRE

Baked Wild Mushrooms with Parmesan

SERVES 4

25g dried porcini
4 handfuls of fresh mushrooms
500ml tub crème fraiche
1 clove garlic – crushed
Parmesan to sprinkle over ramekins
Handful chopped parsley
Knob of butter
Olive oil

Soak the dried porcini, put them into bowl with enough hot water to just cover, leave for

Baked wild mushrooms with Parmesan continued...

half an hour. Quarter the fresh mushrooms and sauté in butter and olive oil with the crushed garlic. Drain the porcini – keeping the juice – and add them to the pan until cooked. Add the crème fraiche and warm through. Throw in a handful of chopped parsley. Put the cooked mushrooms into ramekin dishes with the grated Parmesan on top. Put them into the oven for about 10 minutes to heat up. Serve immediately with warm fresh bread. You can also do this with smoked haddock instead of mushrooms.

Miranda McHardy
BANCHORY, KINCARDINESHIRE

Egg Mousse

SERVES 6

1 tin condensed consommé
Half a sachet of gelatine – dissolved
8 hard boiled eggs
275ml double cream
Freshly ground salt and pepper

Put half the eggs and half the consommé in a liquidiser and process. Pour into a bowl. Now liquidise the remaining eggs and consommé and add to the bowl. Whip the cream lightly. Combine all the ingredients including the dissolved gelatine and seasoning and leave to set in fridge.
    I sometimes add a little curry powder.

Diana Macnab
LEUCHARS, FIFE

Baked Asparagus

MAKES A DELICIOUS STARTER OR LUNCH DISH.
SERVES 4

About 1kg asparagus spears
2 tablespoons olive oil
Coarse salt crystals
2-3 tablespoons balsamic vinegar
100g Parmesan cheese

Heat oven to 220°C, gas mark 7.
Snap off ends of asparagus stalks. Arrange spears in a single layer on a heavy baking tray. Sprinkle over the oil and roll spears round to coat well. Scatter over salt. Bake for 10-15 minutes until spears are just tender. Divide between 4 warm plates and sprinkle over balsamic vinegar and shavings of Parmesan cheese.
    Serve with warm crusty bread and butter.
VARIATION
Serve with free range eggs fried in olive oil for a more substantial lunch dish.

Maureen Wood
TARLAND, ABERDEENSHIRE

Baked Brie with Sun Dried Tomatoes and Pine nuts

SERVES 4

1 round brie (225g)
1 tablespoon sun dried tomatoes in oil
1 tablespoon fresh parsley – chopped
1 tablespoon pine nuts

Preheat oven to 230°C, gas mark 8.

Trim the white rind off the top of the cheese. Spread the tomatoes and parsley evenly over the surface of the cheese and sprinkle with pine nuts. Bake for 10 minutes. Serve with crackers or oatcakes.

Claire Maitland

CRATHES, KINCARDINESHIRE

Italian Roasted Peppers

SERVES 4

4 red peppers – halved and de-seeded
4 cloves garlic – chopped
Basil leaves and/or pesto
8 anchovy fillets – chopped
16-20 cherry tomatoes – halved
1 buffalo mozzarella – torn
8 tablespoon grated Parmesan
Olive oil

Preheat oven to 180°C, gas mark 5.
Put peppers into roasting tin and fill with tomatoes, garlic, basil and/or pesto and anchovies. Dot with mozzarella. Top with Parmesan. Drizzle with olive oil. Roast for 35-40 minutes. Serve with warm ciabatta.

Miranda McHardy

BANCHORY, KINCARDINESHIRE

Asparagus and Egg

PER PERSON

Asparagus – a few stems per person
1 egg
Parmesan cheese
Freshly ground salt and pepper

Trim asparagus and cut into desired size. Hard boil an egg, shell and chop. Fry asparagus on a hot oiled griddle until slightly charred, season with salt and pepper. Mix everything together. Shave thin slices of fresh Parmesan cheese over mixture. Enjoy with good bread.

Dr Noelle Murphy

A & E DEPARTMENT, RAIGMORE, INVERNESS

Camembert en Croute

SERVES 4

1 whole camembert
1 pack of ready rolled puff pastry

Heat oven to 200°C, gas mark 6.
Take a whole camembert and wrap it in a sheet of ready rolled puff pastry.
Bake for around 25 minutes until golden.
Serve in wedges with cranberry sauce and salad. Rich and yummy.

Clare Pelly

EDINBURGH UNIVERSITY

Baked Camembert with Red Onion Marmalade

SERVES 4/6

1 Camembert cheese
1 packet puff pastry
2 red onions – finely chopped
3 tablespoons redcurrant jelly
1 teaspoon brown sugar
1 glass red wine

Heat oven to 200°C, gas mark 6.
Roll pastry until flat (approximately A4 size).
Place camembert in centre of pastry and pull all four corners of the pastry together sealing the cheese in the parcel.
Bake for 20-25 minutes

Red onion marmalade
Brown the onions. Add red wine and reduce. Gradually add the redcurrant jelly and sugar and reduce until stodgy consistency. Serve on bed of salad with marmalade around the outside.
Tip: don't serve it yourself
– let the guests help themselves

Alex Henderson
BURRELTON, PERTHSHIRE

TIP...
Chew parsley to get rid of garlic or onion breath

Simple Garlic Mushroooms

SERVES 4/6

1 large clove garlic
Knob of butter
500g any kind of mushrooms

Crush garlic clove and put in a saucepan with the butter. Just as the butter melts, add the mushrooms and put the lid on the saucepan. Leave until the juices begin to run. Stir and simmer for 2/3 minutes. Serve as a starter with toast or with a large juicy steak.

Renwick Drysdale
KILRIE, FIFE

Asparagus wrapped in Parma Ham

PER PERSON

4 stalks asparagus
2 slices Parma ham
2 tablespoons olive oil
Freshly ground black pepper
1 tablespoon Parmesan cheese shavings

Heat oven to 200°C, gas mark 6.
Wrap stalks of asparagus in 1 piece of Parma ham, then place in a shallow dish. Drizzle in olive oil and season with black pepper. Bake in the oven for 10-15 minutes.
    Place on serving dish and top with Parmesan shavings

Harry Maitland
CRATHES, KINCARDINESHIRE

Chicken Liver Pâté with Green Peppercorns

SERVES 8

450g fresh or frozen chicken livers
110g unsalted butter
1 medium onion – chopped
1 clove garlic – crushed
Good handful chopped fresh thyme/parsley
Salt and pepper
1 tablespoon brandy
1 tablespoon dry sherry
1 or 2 tablespoons green peppercorns
(in brine)

Soften onion and garlic in frying pan, add livers and herbs and cook for 10 minutes. Add the brandy and sherry and cook off the alcohol. Melt butter and put into jug. Place liver mix in a blender and drip butter through spout slowly until mix becomes a fine paste. Tip into bowl and stir through green peppercorns. Pour into serving dish and cover the top with more melted butter. Allow to set. Freezes well.

Lucy Anderson
SUSSEX

Mystery Starter

SERVES 6

225g Philadelphia cream cheese or boursin
1 tin Campbells' beef consommé

Put the cheese into a blender, add half the consommé, season well and blend. (Optional – add teaspoon of curry powder.) Pour into individual ramekins and leave to set in fridge. When ready, pour a little of the remaining consommé on the top of each, set again and serve.

Maurie Jesset
DOUNE, PERTHSHIRE

Chicken Liver Pâté

SERVES 4/6

1 red onion or shallot – chopped
1 clove garlic
75g butter
225g chicken livers
parsley, bay leaf, thyme
1 dessertspoon brandy

Fry onion and garlic in 25g butter and then add chicken livers. Fry for 2-3 minutes. Add herbs and cook a minute longer. Cool and liquidise. Stir in the rest of the butter and brandy. Put in a mould and cover. Chill. Serve with fresh toast and butter

Anne Wolrige Gordon
NEWBURGH, ABERDEENSHIRE

Chilli and Garlic Prawns

SERVES 4

16 raw prawns
2 garlic cloves
1 red chilli
75ml olive oil
pinch of salt

Peel the prawns with a sharp knife. Cut a slit

Chilli and garlic prawns continued...

along back of each prawn and carefully remove the dark vein of each prawn, rinse prawns in cold water and pat dry with kitchen paper.

Peel and crush the garlic and,wearing gloves, deseed and finely slice the chilli.

Heat oil in a large frying pan or wok.

Add the garlic and chilli. Fry gently for about a minute then add the prawns. Fry each side for about 1 minute or until pink and opaque. Season with pinch of salt and serve immediately.

Serve on a small bed of salad.

Lucy Campbell
MARYCULTER, ABERDEENSHIRE

Tuna Paté

SERVES 6/8

2 tins of tuna
1 tub ricotta cheese
1 red onion – finely chopped
2 tablespoons sweet chilli sauce
Dash of Worcestershire sauce
1 tablespoon grainy mustard
Freshly ground salt and pepper

Mix all the ingredients together well and serve.

Rowena Macrae
TRINITY GASK, PERTHSHIRE

Cheats Smoked Mackerel Pâte

SERVES 6

4 smoked mackerel fillets
(with peppercorns if you can get them)
2 tubs fresh sour cream and chive dip
Juice and zest of 1 lemon
Lemon thyme/chives/parsley
Freshly ground pepper

Fork the mackerel until it breaks up into small pieces, add the sour cream, juice and zest of the lemon, lots of black pepper and a good handful of any of the fresh herbs you can get. Mix into a coarse paste, then divide into ramekins, top with fresh herbs and serve with melba toast or crusty brown toast and a slice of lemon.

Suzanne Drysdale
KILRIE, FIFE

Dickson's Delight

SERVES 2

1 can beef consommé
2 fresh eggs
Small quantity of fine thread noodles
Grated Gruyére cheese

Put consommé and noodles into a saucepan and break in the eggs. Heat until eggs are cooked – sprinkle grated Gruyére cheese on top and serve.

Alistair Dickson
DOUNE, PERTHSHIRE

Baked Camembert with Mushrooms, Pesto & Sun Dried Tomatoes

SERVES 4/6

1 round 250g camembert cheese
115g mushrooms – sliced
50g sun dried tomatoes chopped
2 tablespoons pesto sauce

Heat oven to 180°c, gas mark 4.
Fry mushrooms in a little olive oil, add pesto and tomatoes. Cut Camembert in half horizontally. Lay rind side down on small oven proof tray. Spread mushroom mixture over bottom half of cheese. Top with remaining camembert rind side up.
    Bake for 12-15 minutes until cheese is soft and just beginning to melt.

Caroline Gilchrist
DORNOCH, SUTHERLAND

Smoked Haddock Pots

SERVES 6

450g spinach or pak choi
600g smoked haddock, undyed
175ml cream/crème fraiche
1 tablespoon grainy mustard
100g cheddar cheese

Heat oven to 180°c, gas mark 4 .
Cook spinach with a tiny amount of water over a medium heat until its wilted. Chop and season it then divide between 6 ramekins. Cut the smoked haddock into chunks and place on top of the spinach and season with black pepper. Mix cream and mustard together and spoon over haddock. Scatter cheese on top and bake for 15 minutes.
    Serve when golden and bubbling with salad leaves, lemon juice and warm bread.

Marjorie Macpherson Fletcher
KINGUSSIE, INVERNESS-SHIRE

Parmagiana di Melanzane

SERVES 6

2 aubergines
400g tin tomatoes
1 teaspoon cornflour
1 or 2 packets mozzarella cheese
Olive oil
Freshly ground salt and pepper

Heat oven to 180°c Gas mark 4.
Slice aubergines and place in salt water for 10 minutes. Fry them for 7/8 minutes and drain off the oil. Strain the tomatoes and thicken juice with cornflour. Put layers of aubergines in an ovenproof dish, cover with tomatoes, then cheese, and top with the thickened tomato juice. Cook until cheese has melted. Can also be cooked in individual pots/ramekins

Kate Robertson
DRUMBLADE, ABERDEENSHIRE

"

Driving along the A90, a single vehicle overtook me driving at about 90mph. The car clipped the central reservation, flipped over the road into a nearby field coming to rest on its wheels on an electric fence.

As I always carry my Sandpiper Bag in my car I was able to stabilise the 17 year old boy, prior to the arrival of the ambulance. The car was a mangled wreck and the boy was extremely lucky to survive his accident.

There is no doubt that Sandpiper bags make a great deal of difference in these circumstances.

GP, Aberdeen

salads

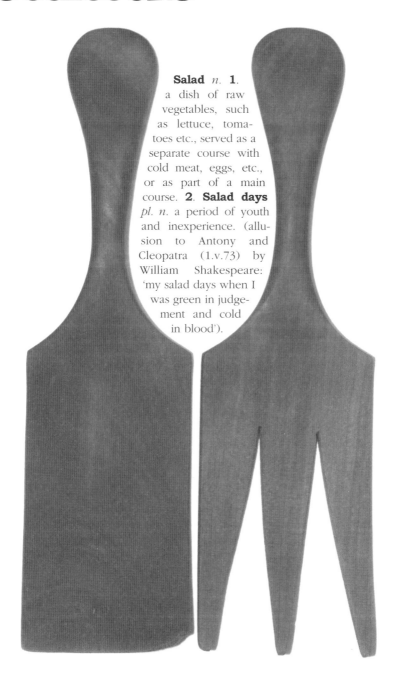

Salad *n.* **1.** a dish of raw vegetables, such as lettuce, tomatoes etc., served as a separate course with cold meat, eggs, etc., or as part of a main course. **2.** **Salad days** *pl. n.* a period of youth and inexperience. (allusion to Antony and Cleopatra (1.v.73) by William Shakespeare: 'my salad days when I was green in judgement and cold in blood').

Artichoke Hearts and Broad Beans in Mint Sauce

SERVES 2/4

1 can artichoke hearts
50g shelled broad beans
Level tablespoon chopped mint
Level teaspoon honey
2 tablespoons malt or wine vinegar

Gently boil the beans for exactly 8 minutes, drain and set aside to cool. Combine the mint and honey and add the vinegar to make a mint sauce (do not be tempted to use a shop bought mint sauce for this). Rinse and drain the artichokes and cut lengthways into quarters. Put into individual bowls with the beans and pour over the sauce. Serve with warm pitta bread and lashings of olive oil.

John Page.
CENTRE FOR NATURAL HEATH, PERTH

Auntie Jenny's Salad

SERVES 2/3

1 x 400g tin chick peas
Half cucumber
2 or 3 tomatoes (9 to 12 cherry tomatoes)
1 or 2 carrots
2cm fresh ginger
1 clove garlic
Light soy sauce
Sweet chilli sauce or rice vinegar
Juice of 1 lime
Coriander

Drain the chick peas and put into a salad bowl. Dice the cucumber and the tomatoes (just halve cherry tomatoes) and add to the bowl. Peel and grate in the carrots and the ginger. Crush the garlic, mix with the soy sauce and the sweet chilli sauce and the juice of the lime. Pour this over the salad and sprinkle with chopped coriander to taste.

Kate Robertson
Drumblade, Aberdeenshire

The Best Pea Salad

SERVES 2/4

Handful black olives
Handful green olives
Handful mint
3 cloves garlic
4cms fresh ginger
Generous dash olive oil
Juice of one lemon
Medium packet of frozen petit-pois or peas

Roughly chop the olives and mint. Finely chop the garlic and the ginger. Add these with the olive oil and lemon juice to the packet of peas in a pan. Warm until the peas are de-frosted. Can be left overnight to gain more flavour.

Nicky Forbes
KEIG, ABERDEENSHIRE

Chicken Club Salad

SERVES 2

1 large bag mixed salad
8 baby tomatoes
1 ripe avocado
2 chicken breasts
4 slices streaky bacon

Wash and spin the salad leaves and tip into a large salad bowl. Cut the tomatoes in half. Peel and slice the avocado and add to the bowl. Either grill or cook the chicken breasts, slice thickly and place on top of the salad. Cook the bacon until crispy and crumble over. Drizzle a good balsamic, or honey and mustard, dressing onto the salad and some toasted pine nuts and toss gently before serving.

Anna Maitland
CRATHES, KINCARDINESHIRE

Hogmanay Salad

SERVES 4

2 bulbs chicory
1 bulb fennel
Handful of watercress
1 red grapefruit
1 yellow grapefruit
Fresh dill sprigs
Good handful of toasted hazelnuts
– chopped roughly

Dressing
Juice of half an orange
Juice of half a lemon
2 to 3 tablespoons olive oil
Freshly ground salt and pepper
chopped fresh dill

Segment the grapefruits carefully and put any spare juice into the dressing. Arrange the chicory leaves, fennel slices, watercress and grapefruit on an ashet or serving plate and sprinkle with hazelnuts and fresh dill sprigs. Drizzle some of the dressing over the salad and serve the remainder in a small jug.

Gillian Vieilledent
LUMPHANAN, ABERDEENSHIRE

Lentil Salad

SERVES 4

1 cup dry lentils
4 whole garlic cloves – peeled and bruised
2 garlic cloves, minced
Quarter teaspoon dried oregano, or thyme
6 tablespoons extra virgin olive oil
6 tablespoons red wine vinegar
Half teaspoon ground cumin
1 small red onion, diced
1 medium red pepper – seeded and diced
3 tablespoons fresh mint – chopped (optional)
170g feta cheese
18 Kalamata olives

Pick over the lentils and discard any stones. Wash lentils and place in a large saucepan with the bay leaves, bruised garlic and oregano. Cover with water by 4cm. Bring to boil, turn down heat and simmer uncovered, for 30 minutes, until tender. Drain and cool.
   To make the vinaigrette, whisk together the olive oil, vinegar, garlic, cumin salt and

Lentil Salad continued...

pepper in a small bowl. Toss the vinaigrette with the lentils, onions, pepper, half a teaspoon of salt and freshly ground back pepper. Let it stand for 20 minutes and add more seasoning to taste. To serve, toss the salad with the mint and place on a platter.

Charlotte Blau
UNIVERSITY OF DUNDEE MEDICAL SCHOOL

Potatoes with Groovy Green Mayonnaise

680g of new potatoes – cooked and cooled
Groovy green mayonnaise
60ml good mayonnaise – *Hellmann's*!
2-3 cloves garlic
100g fresh spinach
Bunch spring onions
60ml olive oil
30ml vinegar
Freshly ground salt and pepper
1 small carton single cream

Stir mayonnaise and cream in bowl. Put the vinegar and oil into a liquidiser, to this add roughly chopped spinach leaves and spring onions. Throw in the garlic and some salt and pepper. Reduce to a purée and mix with the mayonnaise and cream. The sauce will be a coating consistency. If it's too thin, add more mayonnaise. If it is too thick, add cream. This is lovely with summer food such as poached salmon or other 'pink food' like a really good baked ham.

Lucy Gordon
OLD MELDRUM, ABERDEENSHIRE

Puy Lentil Salad

SERVES 4

250ml dry Puy lentils (or 1 large tin)
1 red pepper
10 cherry tomatoes
2 cm fresh ginger
1 leek
Balsamic vinegar
1 bunch coriander – chopped
Butter or olive oil
Freshly ground salt and pepper

Slice the leeks thinly and fry in a little butter until cooked but not coloured. For the last minute of cooking, add the red pepper thinly sliced, to the leeks, just to soften. Cook the Puy lentils, if dried, as per instructions. Drain the lentils and pepper and put into a bowl. Pour the balsamic vinegar over whilst still warm and stir. Grate the ginger into the salad. Add the tomatoes and coriander just before serving and mix well. Season with salt and pepper to taste.

Clare de Winton
FRIOCKHEIM, ANGUS

Rocket and Pine Nut Salad

SERVES 4

1 bag of wild rocket
50g pine nuts
Balsamic vinegar
Extra virgin olive oil
Freshly ground salt and pepper

Toast the pine nuts lightly in a dry pan. Place

the rocket on a large platter or on individual plates. Just before serving sprinkle the pine nuts over the leaves, drizzle with olive oil and balsamic vinegar and season to taste.

Sera Irvine
TARLAND, ABERDEENSHIRE

Loon's Sweet Salad Dressing – utterly scrumbolian…

25ml lemon juice
25ml balsamic vinegar
100ml best virgin olive oil
Small dollop grainy mustard
Small dollop horseradish sauce
Oodles maple syrup
Freshly ground salt and pepper

Lob it all into a screw top jar and shake furiously. Taste the result and find anything green to pour it onto – irresistible!

Alasdair Hilleary – 'Loon'
REDCASTLE, ROSS-SHIRE

Salami, Apple and New Potato Salad with Mayonnaise

SERVES 6

450g good salami in one piece
3 crisp dessert apples (Coxs or Braeburns)
450g Jersey Royal potatoes
2 cloves garlic
6-8 tablespoons good mayonnaise – your own or Tesco's Finest Roasted Garlic Mayonnaise
Freshly ground pepper
Finely chopped parsley

Skin the salami and cut into chunks. Core the apples and cut into 1cm chunks. Cut the potatoes in half if necessary.
   Mix all ingredients together with garlic mayonnaise and grind over some black pepper. Pile the salad into a bowl and sprinkle with chopped parsley. Serve with a tomato and basil salad.

Araminta Dallmeyer
NORTH KESSOCK, ROSS-SHIRE

Sandpiper Chicken Salad

SERVES 4

4 chicken breasts cut into chunky strips
1 red pepper, roasted
1 handful mange tout peas – blanched
1 bag mixed lettuce leaves
Any vegetables you like, peas, broad beans, baby corn
Juice of 1 lemon
2 tablespoons sweet chilli sauce
Good olive oil
Balsamic vinegar

Marinade
1 lemon
1 tablespoon soy sauce
1 clove garlic, crushed
1 teaspoon ground coriander seed
1 teaspoon fresh ginger – finely chopped
2 tablespoons olive oil

Marinate the chicken for at least 1 hour. Barbecue or grill the chicken, or put onto a baking tray in the oven until cooked. Mix with the lemon juice and the sweet chilli sauce and add to the salad. Place the salad on a large flat plate. Arrange all the other ingredients on the top. Drizzle with olive oil and balsamic vinegar and grind some black pepper over. Finally place the chicken on the top - it doesn't matter if it's still warm.

Serve with crusty fresh bread.

Miranda McHardy
BANCHORY, KINCARDINESHIRE

Tasty Crunchy Salad

SERVES 4 AS A STARTER

1 whole floret broccoli – broken into small pieces
1 whole cauliflower – broken into tiny florets
6 pieces streaky bacon
1 red onion
2 stalks celery
Grated cheese of your choice
Dressing of your choice (French, garlic or blue cheese)

Wash broccoli and cauliflower and chop the onion and celery finely and put into salad bowl. Grill the bacon until crispy and then break it into pieces. Sprinkle the bacon and grated cheese over the salad, add dressing and mix well. Serve.

Susan Proctor
DYCE, ABERDEENSHIRE

Seared Smoked Salmon with Apple Salad and Horseradish Cream

SERVES 4 AS A STARTER

4 thick pieces of smoked organic salmon
1 tbsp sunflower oil

Horseradish Cream
40g freshly grated horseradish
90g mayonnaise
90g good crème fraiche
A squeeze of lemon juice
Pinch of salt

Apple and watercress salad
2 medium eating apples skin on – grated
2 spring onions – finely sliced at an angle
150g watercress – thick stalks removed
1 tsp lemon juice
1 tbsp olive oil

Start by making the horseradish cream. In a bowl, mix together the horseradish, mayonnaise, crème fraiche, lemon juice and salt. Set aside. In a bowl, combine the apple, spring onions, watercress, lemon juice and olive oil. Toss everything together using a fork. When almost ready to serve, heat a frying pan over a medium heat, add the sunflower oil and when hot, lay the smoked salmon portions in the pan. Sear for only 30 seconds on each side, remove and drain on kitchen paper. To serve, divide the salad between four plates. Place the salmon next to the salad and dress with a dollop of the horseradish cream. Serve immediately.

Nick Nairn
PORT OF MENTEITH, STIRLING

Thai Beef Salad

SERVES 4/6

A bit of effort is required with all the chopping, but it's well worth it!

3 tablespoons sesame seeds	2 peppers (red, orange or yellow)
2-3 hot chillies	1 cucumber
1-2 garlic cloves	1 red onion
2 large thick rump steaks – each one about 300g	1 lemongrass stalk, sliced
	1 bag mixed salad leaves
Juice of 3 limes	1 handful fresh mint
2 tablespoons soy sauce	1 handful fresh coriander
3 tablespoons sunflower oil	Chilli oil to taste
8 spring onions	Freshly Ground salt and pepper

Finely chop chillies, removing seeds if a milder flavour is preferred. Peel and slice the garlic. Put the steaks into a large shallow dish and sprinkle with the chillies, lime juice and garlic. Mix the soy sauce with 2 tablespoons of the sunflower oil and drizzle over the meat, cover and leave for at least an hour, preferably overnight.

Toast the sesame seeds in a small pan until golden, tossing them constantly. Allow to cool and crush with a pinch of salt using a pestle and mortar.

Trim the spring onions and shred finely. Slice the peppers into thin shreds. Drop both into a bowl of cold water and chill. Halve the cucumber lengthways, scoop out the seeds and cut into thin strips about 5cm long. Cover and chill. Peel and slice the shallots.

Remove the meat from the marinade, reserving the liquid, and scrape off any garlic and chilli. Heat remaining oil in a large pan over a very high heat, add one steak and press down to cook evenly. Turn and repeat on the other side. Lower the heat slightly and cook for a further 2-4 minutes, ideally it should be rare. Repeat with second steak. Slice thinly and put aside.

Add the lemongrass and the marinade to the pan, simmer for 1 minute then pour over the meat. Leave to cool. Combine the lettuce, cucumber and half the drained shredded vegetables in a shallow serving dish. Toss with a little chilli oil and half the sesame seeds. Add the onion, mint and coriander to the beef and pile onto the salad. Top with the remaining vegetables and sesame seeds.

Janey Haig
ASHMANSWORTH
HAMPSHIRE

TIP...
You don't get a second chance to make a first impression

Tomato, Onion and Coriander Salad

SERVES 4/6

225g tomatoes
75g red onion – peeled and chopped
4 tablespoons fresh coriander – chopped
Three quarters teaspoon salt
2 tablespoons lemon juice
Half teaspoon cayenne pepper
Half teaspoon roasted cumin seeds

Cut the tomatoes and chop the onions roughly and put them into a bowl with the other ingredients and mix well. Leave to chill. Serve with barbequed chicken or lamb.

Louisa Leader
GLENCARSE, PERTHSHIRE

Warm Avocado, Bacon and Walnut Salad

SERVES 4/6

1 bag mixed lettuce leaves
2 avocados
4 slices smoked bacon
2 tomatoes
Handful halved walnuts
2 spring onions
3 tablespoons white wine vinegar
9 tablespoons olive oil
1 teaspoon Dijon mustard

Arrange the lettuce on plates. Peel and chop the avocados and tomatoes and place on top of the lettuce with the walnuts. Fry the bacon in a little olive oil and add the sliced spring onions to soften them up. When this is cooked, add some white wine vinegar to bring all the juices from the bottom of the pan. Add some olive oil and mustard and pour the bacon and vinaigrette over the salad whilst still warm.

Lynsey Brunton
ARBROATH, ANGUS

Warm Wild Duck Breast with an Orange Salad and Chocolate and Hazelnut Vinaigrette

SERVES 4

4 wild duck breasts
4 oranges
1 bag lamb's lettuce
50g toasted hazelnuts
2 teaspoons cocoa powder
1 teaspoon honey
200ml hazelnut oil

Season and brush the duck breasts with oil. Gently grill for approximately 4-6 minutes, so that they are still pink inside. Peel the oranges and cut out into segments keeping the juice. Reduce the juice by about half, over a medium heat. Add the honey and cocoa powder then whisk in the oil, chop the hazelnuts roughly and add. Mix the salad with about a quarter of the dressing arrange on a large plate. Slice the duck and place onto the salad, spooning the rest of the dressing over and around the duck.

Castleton House Hotel
GLAMIS, ANGUS

Warm Mushroom and Duck Salad

SERVES 6

4 tablespoons runny honey
3 duck breasts
3 tablespoons fresh orange juice
1 tablespoon red wine vinegar
8 tablespoons olive oil
1 teaspoon whole grain mustard
2 tablespoons Greek yoghurt
1 clove garlic
1 bunch spring onions
650g mixed mushrooms
2 bags lamb's lettuce

Brush honey onto one side of each duck breast and season. Slice the white part of the spring onions and chop the green tops. Grill the duck for 10 minutes, honey side up, until caramelised and then repeat on other side. Rest for 5 minutes and then cut each breast into 6 slices.

Meanwhile, mix together orange juice, vinegar, mustard and yoghurt. Add 5 tablespoons of olive oil and whisk in. Add the chopped green spring onion. Crush the garlic and fry in the remaining oil. Add mushrooms and stir fry for 5 minutes. Remove from heat and drain off any excess liquid. Add the sliced spring onion. Divide lettuce between plates and top with mushrooms and duck slices.

Drizzle over the dressing.

Claire Maitland
CRATHES, KINCARDINESHIRE

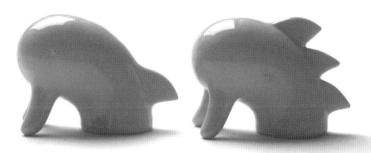

As a Consultant in Accident and Emergency Medicine covering an area which is mainly rural, the Sandpiper Trust has been a godsend. Working with Basics Education Scotland, we have trained our local GPs in immediate care. However, they have always been dependent on using equipment which arrives with the ambulance. In rural areas, a General Practitioner will often be the first attender at emergencies. Training GPs in Immediate Care without supplying them with equipment is a bit like teaching someone to ride a bike and then telling them to walk!

With the introduction of Sandpiper bags and vehicle locators to support training initiatives, we are now increasingly seeing patients arriving from rural communities having been fully resuscitated and pain free. The Sandpiper Trust has contributed to a fundamental improvement in pre- hospital care in Scotland.

A&E Consultant, Aberdeen

vegetables

Vegetable *n.* **1**. any of various herbaceous plants having parts that are used as food, such as peas. beans, cabbage, potatoes, cauliflower and onions.

Miles and miles and miles....

Broccoli travels almost 1000 miles from Spain to the UK.
The traditional English varieties — such as purple sprouting broccoli
— are only available from February to April.
Frozen broccoli has more nutrients than fresh refridgerated imports

Aubergine Bake

SERVES 4

1 aubergine
3 peppers of different colours
2 red onions
6 tomatoes
1 jar pasta sauce (preferably good quality with sun-dried tomatoes)
2 tablespoons olive oil
250g grated mozzarella

Pre-heat oven to 180°C, gas mark 5. Top of Aga baking oven.
Slice the aubergine and put in a large bowl. Sprinkle with salt and leave for an hour then rinse. This gets rid of any bitterness in the aubergine but is not essential if you don't have time. Slice other ingredients and layer in an ovenproof dish with onion first, then peppers, tomatoes and aubergines. Spread pasta sauce on top and drizzle in oil. Cover in foil and bake for an hour and a half. Remove foil and discard, sprinkle with mozzarella and return to oven for another half an hour or until cheese is bubbling and golden. Serve with crusty bread and a crisp green salad. Yum yum.

Carol Bristow
CLATT, ABERDEENSHIRE

Black-eyed Al's Casserole

270g black eyed beans – dried
450g can of plum tomatoes
1 red onion – chopped
1 clove garlic – crushed
90g tomato purée
Half green pepper – diced
600ml water
1 vegetable stock cube
30g fresh parsley – chopped
30g fresh basil – chopped
480g button mushrooms – sliced
300g can of sweetcorn

Cover the beans with cold water and soak overnight. Put the beans in a saucepan with enough fresh water to cover. Bring to the boil and simmer for 30 minutes. Drain. In a large saucepan mix the beans, tomatoes, onion , garlic, tomato purée, chopped pepper and water. Add the vegetable stock cube. Bring to the boil, reduce heat and simmer for one hour, stirring occasionally. Add the parsley, basil, mushrooms and sweetcorn. Mix well and simmer for a further 15 minutes. Serve with hot crusty bread.

Alastair Robertson
DRUMBLADE, ABERDEENSHIRE

TIP...
Put avocado stone in with the avocado (doesn't need to be touching) in the salad or whatever, and it prevents the avocado from going brown. It will stay green for AGES

Quick Potato Dauphinoise

SERVES 6

This can be made and re-heated or frozen. Try adding layers of smoked haddock and sliced tomatoes to make a good supper.

900g Maris Piper potatoes
150ml double cream
350ml milk
salt and pepper
1 clove garlic – crushed
Freshly grated Parmesan cheese

Pre heat oven to 190°C, gas mark 5.
Peel and slice potatoes as thin as possible, do not rinse. Put milk, cream, garlic and potatoes in a saucepan and heat slowly until thick and creamy, stirring all the time. Pour into greased dish, cover in Parmesan and bake for 1 hour until tender.

Vicks Drysdale
CUPAR, FIFE

Baked Mushrooms

Portabella mushrooms
Olive oil
Soya sauce

Mix equal quantities of olive oil and soya sauce and spoon into portabella mushrooms. Cook in a hot oven for 15 to 20 minutes.

Val Rahtz
ECHT, ABERDEENSHIRE

Courgette Fritters

SERVES 10/12

3 medium courgettes – grated
2 medium eggs – separated
150ml double cream
75g plain flour
2 spring onions (chopped finely including all green tops)
Sunflower oil
Sea salt

Mix the courgettes with with 1 tablespoon of salt. Leave to drain for 15-20 minutes in a colander. When most of the juice has run off, wash the courgettes under a tap and squeeze dry with your hands. In a bowl, whisk egg yolks, cream and flour to make smooth batter. Add the courgettes and spring onions to the batter mix.

In separate bowl whisk the egg whites lightly until frothy (not too stiff and dry). Then fold gently into the batter mix.

Heat a teaspoon of oil in a non-stick frying pan and spoon in 3 separate amounts of batter and leave until brown. Turn the fritters over and cook until second side is brown.

Drain on kitchen paper and keep warm. Repeat until all the batter is used up.

Clare de Winton
FRIOCKHEIM, ANGUS

Onion and Mixed Vegetable Quiche

SERVES 6/8

225g frozen mixed vegetables
1 large onion – chopped
500g block of frozen shortcrust pastry
100/125g grated strong cheddar cheese
6 free range eggs made up to 600g by milk
Olive oil

Preheat oven to 200°C, gas mark 6.
Gently fry onion and the frozen vegetables in olive oil until the onion is well coloured and the vegetables look slightly charred.

Butter a 23cm quiche or flan tin and roll out the pastry to fit. Try to make sure that it overlaps as it can shrink a bit while cooking. Prick the base of the pastry and cover with a piece of tin foil. Weigh the foil down with baking beans (if you don't have these, use some dried chickpeas). Put in the oven for about 15 minutes. Take the flan dish out of the oven and remove the beans and tin foil. The sides should look cooked but the base will still be raw looking. Put it back in for further 10 minutes.

Season the eggs and milk mixture well with salt and pepper and mix thoroughly.

Now you just have to layer everything together. Put the fried onions and vegetables into the pastry case and then pour over the egg and milk mixture. Top it with the grated cheese scattered over. Then put it back in hot oven for about 20 minutes before turning oven down to 150°C for another 15 to 20 minutes

Andy Spencer
PARAMEDIC – GLASGOW

Spinach Cheese Pie

SERVES 6

1 packet puff pastry – divided into two
225g feta cheese – crumbled
100g cheddar cheese – grated
2 large eggs – whisked
2 bags of spinach – blanched, drained, pressed as dry as possible, then chopped
Freshly ground salt and pepper
Good pinch of nutmeg
Sesame seeds
1 egg to glaze
26cm flan or quiche dish (metal better than china)

Preheat oven to 190°C, gas mark 5
Defrost pastry. Mix whisked eggs with grated cheddar and crumbled feta (looks like scrambled eggs!). Add salt, pepper and a good pinch of nutmeg. Add chopped spinach (as dry as possible). Roll out just over half the pastry, larger than your tin (which must be very well greased). Put pastry into it and press against the sides. Fill with the egg, cheese and spinach mixture. Roll out second half of pastry and place over top. Brush with egg and sprinkle with sesame seeds. Bake in oven for 25 minutes. Cool. Eat warm (but not hot!) or cold (but not straight from fridge!).

Henrietta Croker Poole
BATTERSEA, LONDON

Dauphinoise Potatoes

SERVES 6

This can be prepared up to oven stage
2 days in advance if kept chilled

Preheat oven to 190°C, gas mark 5

1125g potatoes
1 pint of whipping cream and milk (half and half)
1 clove of garlic – chopped
Lots of pepper and a little salt
75g of Gruyére or Cheddar cheese

Chop garlic and bring to boiling point with cream and milk, leave to infuse. Peel and slice potatoes thinly in mandolin or food processor. Partially cook sliced potatoes in cream and milk mixture until it begins to thicken, stirring all the time to prevent sticking. Put potato mix into oven dish and sprinkle grated cheese on top. Cook for 40 minutes.

Jak Kennedy
CARLOPS, MIDLOTHIAN

TIP...
To keep peeled potatoes from turning brown, add a slice of white bread or lemon juice to the water

White and Green Stuffed Peppers

A vegan treat. A number of ingredients in this recipe are claimed to have aphrodisiac qualities – try it for yourself.

Core and halve as many large green peppers as you are catering for. Par-boiling will help to reduce the roasting time though is not necessary if the peppers are well oiled.

Smear with a good quality olive oil and stuff with your choice from the following white and green ingredients:

Small salad potatoes – par-boiled
Artichoke hearts (prepared from a deli are ideal)
Sliced palm hearts (from a can)
Mini sweet corn cobs
Sliced courgettes par-fried in oil
Sweet garden peas
Broad beans, ideally skinned
Asparagus tips

Cover with a green pesto dressing (if cooking for a vegan avoid those pre-prepared with Parmesan or Pecorino), season and sprinkle with pine nuts to taste.
    Oven roast until cooked – 15 minutes in a moderate oven is usually sufficient

Andrew Marsden
SCOTTISH AMBULANCE SERVICE – EDINBURGH

An adaptable Frittata

SERVES 4

Great with a fresh green salad and glass of Rosé. In the winter you can use root vegetables like beetroot, carrot, parsnip etc.

6 free range eggs
1 large or two small red onions
1 clove of garlic chopped
2 tablespoons olive oil
75g goat's cheese or other cheese kicking around in fridge
Broccoli – few stems – or any vegetables
6/8 boiled new potatoes or sweet potatoes
Sea salt
Handful of fresh herbs if available – basil or coriander – if no fresh available just a pinch of mixed herbs will do.

Preheat oven to 170°C, gas mark 4.
Crack eggs into a bowl and give a whisk for a few minutes and season well. Chop the onion, no need for ultra finely sliced – this is a quick and rustic frittata. Pour olive oil in a frying pan, throw in onions and garlic and sauté for 10 minutes. Add the vegetables in bite size chunks and cook for a few minutes. Mix well and pour into a Pyrex dish. Pour the beaten eggs over the vegetable mix in the oven dish. Cut up the (sweet) potatoes into rustic chunks and add to the dish. Break up a small round of goat's cheese and crumble into the mixture or grate a chunk of hard cheese in to mix. Add the fresh or dried herbs. Stir and place in oven for 25-30 minutes or until brown and bubbling on top. Check after 20 minutes.

Chris and Susie Tiso
MILNATHORT, PERTHSHIRE

Creamy Garlic Cabbage

SERVES 4

Very quick and easy and tastes superb! Goes well with chicken, pheasant, cold beef. Sure to convert any who don't like cabbage normally!

Half a cabbage (savoy, green etc – not red!)
3 cloves garlic
4 tablespoons olive oil
Salt and pepper to taste.
100ml double cream

Slice the cabbage into thin slices. Heat the olive oil in a heavy based pan. Add the garlic and simmer, stirring, so the garlic does not burn. Add the cabbage and stir. Heat over a low heat so as not to burn the cabbage for approx 5 minutes. Add a little more oil if needed. When the cabbage has softened, season and continue to cook for a few more minutes. Add cream as desired, stir well until cream is hot and serve.

Charlotte Waugh
SELKIRK, BORDERS

Greek Spinach Rice Spanakorizi

SERVES 4

500g spinach washed
Half cup long grain rice
1 medium onion
1 clove garlic – finely chopped
1 tablespoon olive oil
1 lemon
Salt and pepper

In a pot with (ideally transparent) lid, glaze onion and garlic, then add rice. Add water (ratio of rice to water 1:2.5) Stir thoroughly. Add spinach on top and put lid on. Reduce heat to lowest setting. Some 30 minutes later, the rice will be cooked and will have absorbed all water. Season with salt and pepper, mix and serve liberally with lemon juice. Decorate with lemon wedge.

Dr Peter Raff
DRUMMORE, STRANRAER

Tomato and Basil Clafoutis

SERVES 4/6

4 eggs
200ml carton crème fraiche
25g plain flour
1 tub cherry tomatoes – halved
4 tablespoons milk
50g grated Parmesan
Good handful fresh basil – torn roughly

Preheat oven to 190°C, gas mark 5. Lightly grease a gratin dish roughly 23cm and 4cm deep. Spread tomatoes on the base. Beat eggs in bowl, then beat in flour, crème fraiche and milk until batter is smooth. Stir in basil and all but one tablespoon Parmesan. Pour batter into dish over tomatoes sprinkle remaining cheese Bake for 20 minutes until puffed up and golden on top. Like a quiche but easier and without the base –can also be eaten cold

Jeanette Ogilvie
GUTHRIE, ANGUS

Couscous and Roasted Vegetables

SERVES 6/8

1 tablespoon butter
1 teaspoon cumin
1 teaspoon ground coriander
1 teaspoon cinnamon
300ml chicken stock
250g couscous
4 tablespoons olive oil
1 red pepper – roughly chopped
1 red onion – sliced into wedges
1 courgette – sliced
12 button mushrooms – halved
2 tablespoons coriander – chopped
Juice of half a lemon

Preheat oven to 200°C, gas mark 5. Toss pepper, onions, courgette and mushrooms in olive oil. Place in an ovenproof dish and roast for 10-15 minutes until tender Melt butter in saucepan, add cumin, coriander and cinnamon and fry gently for 1 minute. Add chicken stock and bring to the boil. Take off heat, add couscous and leave covered for 5 minutes. Fluff up the couscous with fork and add lemon juice, coriander and roasted vegetables. Mix well and serve. Can add cooked chicken, lamb or any cooked meat.

Dr Faye Hamill
ISLE OF ARRAN

Dahl Baht and Tibetan Barley Bread

SERVES 4

I've spent some time travelling in Nepal, and recently spent a couple of weeks there working as an expedition doctor. On each occasion I survived almost exclusively on the food of the Sherpas – Dahl Baht and Tibetan Bread, both of which I grew to love. They are both very tasty and at the same time full of energy giving carbohydrates. Whilst the Dahl at 19,000ft is slightly more basic than the recipe below, it is still very straightforward to make.

The typical breakfast and dinner meal throughout Nepal is Dahl Baht – white rice and lentil soup, curried vegetable, and achar (chutney) and for many Nepalis, it's the only meal they eat, twice a day, everyday! There are many types of Dahl Baht, each slightly different in taste and texture, though the most common includes cauliflower and potatoes. It is often served on a steel plate divided into compartments – the rice in one compartment, the Dahl in another, and the curry (terkari) in a third.

Dahl (lentils)
3-4 cups lentils
3-4 cups water
Half onion
2-3 cloves of garlic, chopped
Half tablespoon ginger
1-2 chilli peppers
1 teaspoon turmeric
1 teaspoon salt

Baht (rice)
1 and half cups Basmati rice
3 cups of water

Tibetan Barley Bread
4 cups flour
2 tablespoons baking powder
2 cups water

Terkari (curry)
4-5 large potatoes – peeled
1 large bunch cauliflower
1 onion – chopped
3-4 tomatoes
4-5 cloves of garlic – chopped
1 and half tablespoons ginger
1-2 chilli peppers
1 and half teaspoons turmeric
1 teaspoon salt
1 teaspoon black pepper
1 and half teaspoons curry powder
1 teaspoon cumin seeds
Plus anything else you need
– spring onions, green beans, peas, carrots.

TIP...
Everyone has attitude, everyone needs attitude, but not everyone has the attitude they need

First you need to make the Dahl
Wash lentils, bring water to boil and add lentils and turmeric. Boil about 1 hour stirring occasionally. About 30 minutes into cooking the dahl, start cooking the rice and the curry (see below). While lentils are boiling, separately fry the chopped onions, garlic, salt and chilli peppers. When lentils start to dissolve, add fried mixture and serve with rice and curry.

For the curry
Start by boiling the potatoes and then set aside. Fry chopped onion, ginger, garlic, salt and chilli peppers until the onion starts to caremelise. Add cauliflower, and stir and cook for 5-6 minutes – add other vegetables at this point if wished. Then add tomatoes, salt, black pepper and curry powder. Mix. After tomatoes have liquefied, add cooked potatoes and cook until the curry is warm and serve

For the bread
Mix the flour and a little water very well by hand and keep adding water until you can make a smooth ball of dough. Then knead the dough very well until the dough is soft. Separate the dough into eight pieces and roll them into ball shapes. Then leave the dough balls in a container with a lid on for 15-20 minutes. After that, place one of the ball shapes on a flat surface and roll it out with a rolling pin, making a flat, round shape about 1-2 cms high. Repeat with all your dough. Heat oil or butter in a frying pan until hot, turn down the heat, put the bread in the pan and cover it with lid. Cook 15 minutes on medium heat. Turn over the bread every 4 or 5 minutes so both sides of bread get well-cooked.

The experience of a lifetime came along when I was invited to travel to Nepal as a doctor for the BBC Extreme Dreams Programme.

The Sandpiper Bag was an invaluable resource to me as an expedition doctor. Its Tardis-like qualities enabled me to carry all the equipment to support a team of over 60 people in the wilderness for a number of weeks. I treated not just the contestants, but also the crew, porters and many of the locals en-route (including home visits!) and it came into its own when I needed to resuscitate a contestant prior to helicopter evacuation.

The bag was genuinely a life-saver and it is perfect for trekking – weighing 20kgs when fully equipped. Equally as invaluable was Bibi, the hardy Sherpa, (a runner up in the Everest Marathon!) who carried it for me when the going got tough.

I could not have done all this without the help of the Sandpiper Trust.

Dr Mike Steven
BANCHORY, KINCARDINESHIRE

Elaine's Veggie Chilli

SERVES 4

2 large onions
3 tablespoons olive oil
2 tins chopped tomatoes
1 tin drained kidney beans
1 tin drained black-eyed beans
1 tin drained aduki beans
Small pack of baby sweetcorn – sliced
1 yellow pepper – seeded and cubed
2 peppers – 1 green, 1 red
2 big squirts tomato puree
2 teaspoons sugar
Chilli powder (to your taste)

Fry onions in olive oil until soft. Add peppers and sweetcorn and cook for a further 5 minutes. Add chilli powder, pepper, sugar and tomato purée. Add tins of tomatoes and cook for approx 15-20 minutes (don't overcook the vegetables). Add beans and cook for a further 5 minutes. Serve on warm plates with brown rice and grated cheese.

Elaine Wallace
CULTS, ABERDEENSHIRE

Carrot and Parsnip Casserole

Place 2 tablespoons of butter in heavy casserole. Peel and slice carrots and parsnips into long thin strips. Place in casserole, cover with lid and put in oven at 180°c for 1 hour – 1 hour 20 minutes.

Pat Norris
MONTREAL, CANADA

Roast Parsnips

SERVES 4

4 medium sized parsnips
Sesame Oil
Semolina

Preheat oven to 200°C, gas mark 6.
Cut each parsnip into 4 long strips and dip into the oil then the semolina. Put them in a roasting tray. Season. Cover with foil and cook for an hour or until crisp but soft inside.

Ruby Mackay
CHALMERS MACKAY MUSIC SCHOOL
INVERURIE, ABERDEENSHIRE

Grilled Avocados

SERVES 8

4 large ripe avocados
2 red skinned apples – quartered
2 celery stalks – finely sliced
4 tablespoons mayonnaise
175g Gruyére cheese – grated
175g cooked prawns
Freshly ground salt and pepper

Cut each avocado in half and remove stone. Scoop out flesh in neat spoonfuls, place in mixing bowl and set aside skins. Add celery, apples, prawns and mayonnaise to avocado. Season well and stir thoroughly. Refill skins with mixture and sprinkle cheese on top, put under very hot grill until cheese turns golden and serve immediately.

Maurie Jesset
DOUNE, PERTHSHIRE

Vegetable Couscous

SERVES 4/6

1 cup of parboiled couscous
1 knob butter
1 can chopped tomatoes 400g
1 can chick peas – drained and washed
1 eggplant, cut into cubes
1 medium onion – coarsely chopped
1 clove garlic, chopped
3 teaspoons olive oil
2 stalks celery – chopped
1 bunch runner beans – chopped
1 pinch chilli (cayenne pepper)
Freshly ground salt and pepper

Glaze onion and garlic in oil, add chopped celery, runner beans, eggplant and chickpeas. Add chopped tomatoes from can and half of the water from washing out the tomato can, season with salt, pepper and chilli pepper. Simmer on medium heat for some 45 minutes.

Add boiling water to couscous (as per package instructions, usually 1 part of boiling water on 1 part of couscous) stir in a knob of butter with a fork and break up any lumps.

Serve immediately with the vegetables in the crater of the heap of couscous.

Dr Peter Raff
DRUMMORE, STRANRAER

Russian Beetroot Salad

SERVES 4

8 small fresh beetroots (use the leaves like spinach for a different dish, very tasty.)
1 cup soured cream
Half cup of crème fraiche (mix with soured cream)
1 tablespoon of vegetable oil
Freshly ground salt and pepper

Boil beetroots until cooked, drain and peel when cooled down enough to handle.
Cut into slices or wedges. Season with salt and pepper and oil. Serve with soured cream which has been enriched by mixing with crème fraiche (imitating Russian 'smetana').

Another variant is replacing the soured cream with a vinaigrette made from 3 stalks of spring onions, 3 cloves garlic, all very finely chopped, walnut oil, vinegar, salt and pepper.

Dr Peter Raff
DRUMMORE, STRANRAER

TIP...
To ripen avocados quickly put them in a bag with a banana or two

Quorn Enchiladas

SERVES 4

Packet of Quorn mince (fresh or frozen)
1 large onion – chopped
Large pack of cherry tomatoes – halved
2 jars of Dorito salsa sauce
1 teaspoon cumin, paprika and chilli flakes
6 tortilla wraps
Freshly ground salt and pepper (red/black)
Olive oil
1 pint of vegetable stock
1 can of refried beans
200g Cheddar cheese
Freshly chopped parsley

Preheat oven to 180°C, gas mark 4.
Heat up oil and fry the onions gently, add the cumin, paprika and chilli flakes – leave to sweat for 5-10 minutes. Add the Quorn mince and cook for 5 minutes, add half of the cherry tomatoes and simmer for about 10 minutes. Gradually add the vegetable stock and reduce (this should take about 15 minutes). Season. Meanwhile layer the bottom of large ovenproof dish with the refried beans. Put the Quorn mixture onto the tortilla wraps, roll and fold, then place on top of the beans. Scatter the chopped cherry tomatoes and the salsa sauce on top (making sure all of the wraps are covered). Sprinkle with lots of Cheddar cheese and parsley. Bake for 20 minutes or until the cheese is melted.

Serve with lovely garlic bread, sour cream and chives dip and crunchy salad. HEY PRESTO ! ENJOY! Hope you understand the recipe... after all I'm no Delia!

Sue Cumming
ABERDEEN

Red Cabbage

SERVES 6/8

1 medium sized red cabbage
2 large cooking apples or 4-6 eating apples
1 large onion
1 tablespoon olive oil
6 tablespoons red wine vinegar
One and a half tablespoons water
1 tablespoon granulated sugar
Half teaspoon ground cloves
Salt and freshly ground black pepper
3 large tablespoons redcurrant jelly

Wash, drain and shred the red cabbage, discarding any coarse outer leaves. Slice the onion and cook in the olive oil in a saucepan until softened. Add the red cabbage and sliced apples in layers. Sprinkle on the sugar (if you use sweet eating apples cut down on quantity). Add the ground cloves and then the wine vinegar and water. Cover with a lid and bring gradually to the boil over a gentle heat. Stir thoroughly and continue cooking over a gentle heat for one and a half to two hours stirring from time until the cabbage is cooked. Season with salt and freshly ground black pepper. Stir in the redcurrant jelly and reheat for 5 to 10 minutes. This can be prepared in advance and reheated and can be served either hot or cold.

Cassandra Whittall
FETTERNEAR, ABERDEENSHIRE

Curry Sauce Recipe

SERVES 4/6

Quick, foolproof and infinitely adaptable. This sauce takes about the same time
to cook as rice so can start them at the same time

1 onion
1 clove garlic or garlic paste
Cooking oil
1 tin chopped tomatoes
6 teaspoons curry powder – or make your own which tastes much better, thus:

> 2 teaspoons cumin
> 1 teaspoon coriander
> 1 teaspoon turmeric
> 1 teaspoon cardomom pods – crushed
> Half teaspoon ginger
> Half teaspoon cinnamon
> Half teaspoon cloves
> Cayenne pepper to taste
> Whole spices ground up taste even better
> Freshly ground salt and pepper

Chop onion and garlic finely and fry slowly in a saucepan till clear and soft
Stir in spice powder and stir for half a minute. Add tinned tomatoes and stir.
Salt and pepper to taste. Bring to boil for a minute or two and it is ready.

You can use this as a base for a variety of dishes...

Chicken
Chop breasts into pieces and simmer in the sauce for 20 minutes.

Chickpeas
Add contents of drained tin and heat.

Lentils
Need to soften by simmering in water for half an hour then mixing in.

Any root vegetable
Cook by boiling first to soften.

Any soft vegetable
eg courgettes, sweet peppers chopped up and simmered for 10 minutes.

Sweet and sour option
Add 2 tablespoons vinegar and something sweet – 1 tablespoon brown sugar, sweet chutney, jam, dried fruit.

Classy finish
Slowly stir in natural yoghurt at the end of cooking, a little at a time, stir well over a low heat.

Dr Andrew Cooper
BIXTER, SHETLAND

Blueprint for achievement

believe... while others are doubting

plan... while others are playing

study... while others are sleeping

decide... while others are delaying

prepare... while others are daydreaming

begin... while others are procrastinating

work... while others are wishing

save... while others are wasting

listen... while others are talking

smile... while others are frowning

commend... while others are criticising

persist... while others are quitting

Electric shock

The recommended first aid for someone who has received a
severe electrical shock has three major components
1. Call for help (999)
2. Make sure the victim is no longer in contact with
the electrical current source. Turn off all power if
this can be done quickly. Do not touch casualty
until electrical source has been disconnected.
3. Check for breathing and heart beat and apply cardiopulmonary resuscitation,
if necessary.

Burns and Scalds

First aid for burns and scalds
* Cool the burnt area immediately with cool water (preferably running water) for at
  least 20 minutes. For example, put the burnt area under a running tap. A shower or
  bath is useful for larger areas. Note: do not use very cold water or ice.
* Remove rings, bracelets, watches, etc, from the affected area. These may cause
  tightness or constriction if any swelling occurs.
* After cooling, remove clothing from the burnt area. However, do not try to pull off
  clothing that has stuck to the skin. This may cause damage.
* A cold compress such as a tea towel soaked in cold water may be soothing over the
  burnt area. You can apply this after the initial cooling under cool water.
* Before going to hospital or to a doctor's surgery, cover the burn with cling film or a
  clean plastic bag and leave it on until seen by a doctor or nurse. Apply cling film in
  layers rather than round like a bandage to prevent it causing pressure if the burnt
  area swells.
* Paracetamol or Ibuprofen may help to ease pain for small burns.

DO NOT prick any blisters.
DO NOT apply creams, ointments, oils, grease, etc
DO NOT put on an adhesive, sticky, or fluffy dressing.

Choking first aid Adult or child over 1 year

A choking person's airway may be completely or partially blocked. A complete blockage is an urgent medical emergency. A partial obstruction can quickly become life threatening if the person loses the ability to breathe in and out sufficiently. Without oxygen, permanent brain damage can occur in as little as 4 minutes. Rapid first aid for choking can save a life. The universal distress signal for choking is grabbing the throat with one or both hands

DO NOT perform first aid if the person is coughing forcefully and able to speak – a strong cough can dislodge the object on its own.

1. Ask the person:
   "Are you choking?"
   "Can you speak?"

If the obstruction is severe:
- Give up to 5 back blows
- Look inside the mouth and remove anything causing an obvious obstruction

If the obstruction has not moved:
- Give up to 5 abdominal thrusts
- Look inside the mouth and remove anything causing an obvious obstruction
- Continue thrusts until the object is dislodged or the person loses consciousness.

If the person becomes unconscious, lower person to the floor, call 999, and begin CPR.

Recovery position
If an adult is unconscious but breathing, place them on their side in the recovery position – see pictures on opposite page.

1. Place arm nearest to you at a right angle.
2. Move other arm, as shown, with the back of their hand against their cheek. Then get hold of the knee furthest from you and pull up until foot is flat on the floor.
3. Pull the knee towards you, keeping the person's hand pressed against their cheek, and position the leg at a right angle.
4. Make sure that the airway remains open by tilting the head back and lifting the chin, and check breathing.

Monitor the casualty's condition until help arrives.

Fitting (seizures)

Usually when a person has an epileptic seizure there is no need to call an ambulance. However you should always dial 999 if:
- It is the person's first seizure
- They have injured themselves badly
- They have trouble breathing after the seizure has stopped
- One seizure immediately follows another with no recovery in between
- The seizure lasts two minutes longer than is usual for them, or
- The seizure lasts for more than five minutes and you do not know how long their seizures usually last.

What to do during the seizure:
- Try to stay calm
- Note the time to check how long the seizure is going on
- Move objects, such as furniture away from the person if there is a risk of injury. Only move the person if they are in a dangerous place; for example, at the top of stairs or in the road
- Put something soft (like a jacket or cushion) under their head, or cup their head in your hands, to stop their head hitting the ground
- Do not restrain them, allow the seizure to happen
- Do not put anything in their mouth – there is no danger of them swallowing their tongue during the seizure

What to do when the jerking (convulsing) has stopped (recovery):
- Roll them on to their side into the recovery position (see below)
- Wipe away any spit and if their breathing is difficult check their mouth to see that nothing is blocking their airway, like food
- Try to minimise any embarrassment. If they have wet themselves deal with this as privately as possible
- Stay with them, giving reassurance, until they have fully recovered

Some people recover quickly after these seizures but more often the person will be very tired, may want to sleep and may not feel 'back to normal' for several hours or sometimes days.

Febrile Convulsions

A febrile convulsion is a seizure (a 'fit') which occurs in some children when they have a fever (high temperature). The vast majority of febrile convulsions are not serious. Full recovery with no permanent damage is usual.

Recognition:
- Hot skin that may appear red and flushed, with a very hot forehead
- Twitching muscles and their eyes may appear fixed or roll upwards
- Arching of back and clenched fists
- Holding breath with a blue-looking face

What to do:
- Your main aim is to ensure the child doesn't injure themselves, and to cool them down
- Remove any clothing and open the window
- Use tepid water to sponge over the child – they will start to become more alert DO NOT put the child into a bath of cold water
- The convulsion will stop once they have cooled down
- If the child suffers a prolonged convulsion seek medical advice

Once recovered encourage the child to drink water and give Paracetamol syrup to help reduce temperature

Stroke

Stroke is caused by an interruption of the blood supply to the brain. This can be caused by a blood clot or a breaking blood vessel. Nearby brain cells are killed by the stroke, producing impaired bodily control. Strokes are more common in older people but can happen at any age.

Symptoms

- Numbness of face, arm or leg (possibly just one side of the body)
- Difficulty communicating
- Impaired vision in one or both eyes
- Loss of coordination or balance
- Sudden headache
- Flushed face
- Drooping mouth, dribbling, slurred speech
- Loss of bladder or bowel control

Action if casualty is conscious

- Call an ambulance immediately
- Lie casualty down with their head and shoulders raised slightly and supported
- Incline casualty's head to one side and place a cloth to catch any dribbling

Action if casualty is unconscious

- Open an airway and check for breathing
- If the casualty isn't breathing, prepare for resuscitation
- Call 999 immediately.

Suspect a stroke? Act FAST

The Stroke association has a new 'FAST' campaign

Symptoms

The Stroke Association has funded research into FAST – the Face Arm Speech Test – which is used by paramedics to diagnose stroke prior to a person being admitted to hospital.

What is FAST? – FAST requires an assessment of three specific symptoms of stroke.
- Facial weakness - can the person smile? Has their mouth or eye drooped?
- Arm weakness – can the person raise both arms?
- Speech problems – can the person speak clearly and understand what you say?
- Test all three symptoms

Anaphylaxis: first aid

Anaphylaxis is a severe allergic reaction – the extreme end of the allergic spectrum. The whole body is affected, often within minutes of exposure to the allergen but sometimes after hours. Causes of anaphylaxis include peanut and nut allergy, insect stings, latex and drugs, but on rare occasions there may be no obvious trigger.

Symptoms
- Generalised flushing of the skin
- Nettle rash (hives) anywhere on the body
- Sense of impending doom
- Swelling of throat and mouth
- Difficulty in swallowing or speaking
- Severe asthma
- Abdominal pain, nausea and vomiting
- Sudden feeling of weakness
- Collapse and unconsciousness

If you've had an anaphylactic reaction in the past, carry any prescribed medications with you. Epinephrine is the most commonly used drug for severe allergic reactions. If you observe someone having an allergic reaction with signs of anaphylaxis:
1. Call 999
2. Check for special medications that the person might be carrying to treat an allergic attack, such as an auto-injector of Epinephrine (for example, EpiPen). Administer the drug as directed – usually by pressing the auto-injector against the person's thigh and holding it in place for several seconds. Massage the injection site for 10 seconds to enhance absorption. If your doctor prescribed an auto-injector of Epinephrine, read the instructions before a problem develops and also have your household members read them. After administering Epinephrine, have the person take an antihistamine pill if he or she is able to do so.
3. Have the person lie still on his or her back with feet higher than the head.
4. Loosen tight clothing and cover the person with a blanket. Don't give anything to drink.
5. If there are no signs of circulation (breathing, coughing or movement), begin CPR.

Bleeding

With all types of bleeding, it's important to stop the flow of blood as quickly as possible.

Small cuts
Small cuts in veins stop bleeding and clot within a few minutes. The area should then be washed, and a plaster placed gently on top.

Deeper cuts
Deeper cuts in the veins produce dark blood that seeps out slowly and steadily. It can be stopped by gentle pressure on the wound with a sterile or clean cloth, followed by the application of a clean or sterile bandage.

Often, these wounds need sewing or glueing, and therefore medical treatment will be necessary after first aid.

Arterial bleeding
Bleeding from an artery can cause death within a few minutes, so urgent first aid is essential. This type of bleeding pulsates and squirts blood as the pulse beats. The blood is often a light red colour.

To stop bleeding from an artery:
- Apply hard pressure on the wound and keep this up until the patient receives medical treatment
- Press with a sterile cloth or just use your hand if nothing else is available
- Put a bandage on the wound if possible. If the blood soaks through the bandages, press harder until the bleeding stops
- Do not remove the soaked bandages, but place another on top if necessary
- Do not attempt to clean the wound

The person must be made to lie down, preferably with their head lower than the rest of their body. This will ensure that enough oxygen gets to the brain.
If possible, position the wounded area higher than the rest of their body so that the pressure, and therefore the bleeding, will be reduced.

Meningitis

Meningitis is a potentially serious illness that can affect anyone. The term is used to describe a swelling of the tissue that surrounds the brain. This can be the result of a bacterial or viral infection. Always seek medical help if you suspect meningitis.

Recognition:
- High temperature
- Feel drowsy
- Headache
- Sensitive to light
- Show flu-like symptoms
- Vomit
- Stiff neck
- Red or purple rash

Babies may be:
- Floppy
- Listless
- Reluctant to feed

What to do
- You can carry out a very simple test to help you to differentiate between a meningitis rash and any other rash. This test is called the 'glass test'.
- Place a tumbler type drinking glass over the child's rash and apply pressure. In most cases the rash will disappear. In the case of meningitis the red or purple colour rash will remain.

- Check for signs and symptoms described above.
- Seek medical advice immediately.
- Keep the child comfortable somewhere cool.
- Bathe the child's forehead with a damp sponge or flannel.

pasta & rice

...and literally

Spaghetti
Little pieces
of string
Fusilli
Spiral corkscrew
Penne
Pens
Tagliatelle
Cut into strips
Farfalle
Butterfly
Tortellini
Torchered shape

Pasta *n*. any of several variously shaped edible preparations made from a flour and water dough, such as spaghetti. (Italian, from Late Latin: PASTE)

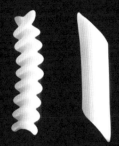

Rice n. **1**. an erect grass, *Oryza sativa*, that grows in East Asia on wet ground and has dropping flower spikes and yellow oblong edible grains that become white when polished. **2**. the grain of this plant. - *vb*. **3**. (tr.) *US and Canadian*. to sieve (potatoes or other vegetables) to a coarse mashed consistency, esp. with a ricer.

Simple Pasta Dish

This is really good for using up left over salmon and smoked salmon bits.

Penne pasta is best
Smoked salmon pieces or hot smoked salmon is even better
and/or cooked salmon
and/or cooked prawns
Créme fraiche
Peas
Chives and parsley
Lemon juice
Knob of butter
Asparagus tips – optional
Tabasco – optional
Freshly ground salt and black pepper

Cook up the penne as instructions and cook the peas. Then, over a gentle heat, simply combine all of the ingredients to your taste. You can add other things, like spring onions or watercress to give it colour. Serve with a green salad. Simple and always a winner.

Diana Sharp
ROTHIEMAY, ABERDEENSHIRE

Easy Peasy Pasta Sauce

SERVES 2

This sauce is also great as a base for Pizza!

1 tin chopped tomatoes
1 whole medium onion
2 cloves garlic – crushed
Half teaspoon sugar
1 dessertspoon tomato purée

Pinch chilli powder
or hot paprika (optional)!
Your favourite pasta
Parmesan cheese

Pour a good slug of olive oil into a pan and add onion and crushed garlic, stirring gently until they soften. Add tomatoes, sugar (which neutralises the acidity of the tomatoes), tomato purée and/or chilli /paprika. Give the whole thing a good stir and let it bubble away on a lowish heat for at least twenty minutes so all the flavours amalgamate.

Add the sauce to the pasta of your choice, tagliatelle, spaghetti, rigatone and give it a good mix. Sprinkle some Parmesan cheese on top and tuck in!

Jenny Tait
LONDON

Tomato Sauce

PROBABLY SERVES 4 WITH PASTA

Quickest tomato pasta sauce and better than any ready made.

1 tin plum tomatoes
Half stock cube or 1 teaspoon stock powder
2 teaspoons dark brown sugar
Dash olive oil
Freshly ground salt and black pepper

Heat all the ingredients in a saucepan, mashing out tomatoes if not ready chopped.

Julia Linzee-Gordon
CLUNY, ABERDEENSHIRE

Macaroni Cheese Variation

SERVES 2/4

225g macaroni or pasta shapes – cook as per instructions in salted water with a bit of oil added
4 slices ham
110g Cheddar cheese
Tomato Sauce
2 tablespoons olive or sunflower oil
1 onion – chopped finely
2 garlic cloves – finely chopped
1 teaspoon oregano
1 tin chopped tomatoes
1 cup white wine or chicken or vegetable stock (if vegetarian}

Preheat oven to 180°C, gas mark 8.
Soften onion and garlic in oil, add tomatoes, oregano and stock or wine. Season with salt and pepper and simmer for about twenty minutes. Add to macaroni.
Chop up the ham and add to macaroni.
Top with grated cheese and bake for half an hour or until bubbling with cheese melted and crisping on top.

If you fancy a slightly spicier version, add a chilli or some chilli paste to the sauce after you have softened the onions, let it cook for a couple of minutes before adding the rest of the ingredients.

Juliette Paton
GRANDHOME, ABERDEEN

Spaghetti with Prawns and Rocket

SERVES 4

455g dried spaghetti
Extra virgin olive oil
2 cloves of garlic – crushed
400g peeled prawns
1 small glass of white wine
2 heaped tablespoons sun dried tomato purée
Juice of 1 lemon
Half a teaspoon of chilli powder
2 handfuls of rocket, roughly chopped
Freshly ground salt and black pepper

Cook the spaghetti in a large pan according to the instructions on the packet and drain it into a colander.

Meanwhile, heat 3 tablespoons of olive oil in a large frying pan and add the garlic and chilli powder. As the garlic begins to colour, add the prawns and cook for 1 minute. Add the white wine and tomato purée and simmer for a couple of minutes. Toss the spaghetti with the sauce, squeeze in the lemon, add half the chopped rocket and season.

Divide between four plates and sprinkle with the rest of the rocket leaves.

Caroline Campbell
BARCALDINE, ARGYLL

Butternut Squash Risotto

SERVES 2/4
DEPENDING ON WHO'S EATING
AND HOW HUNGRY THEY ARE

250g risotto rice (Riso Gallo organic is always good)
700ml hot vegetable stock – about 2 cubes
1 medium butternut squash
Big handful of grated Parmesan, plus extra
handful of sage leaves (you can use spring onion instead) – roughly chopped

Tip the rice into a large microwaveable bowl and add 500ml of the hot vegetable stock. Cover with clingfilm and microwave on high for 5 minutes.

Peel and cut the butternut squash into medium chunks – not too big or it won't soften. Stir the rice and add the butternut squash and the rest of the stock. Cover again with clingfilm and microwave for another 15 minutes, stirring halfway through.

The stock should just about be all absorbed and the rice and squash tender. Let the risotto sit for 2 minutes, then stir the Parmesan and sage or spring onion.

Serve topped with more grated Parmesan.

There you go – 5 ingredients and you have healthy, vitamin C, hassle-free, comfort food – and it makes you popular with the girls (well some) in my experience!

Brian Carlin
BASICS SCOTLAND, SANDPIPER HOUSE
AUCHTERARDER, PERTHSHIRE

Sassy's Green Pasta Sauce

SERVES AS MANY AS YOU LIKE

I freeze this in small quantities as its a very useful standby. Every 'brew' varies!

Spinach
Cream, créme fraiche or cream cheese
Strong cheese
Nutmeg
Freshly ground salt and pepper
Optional Bacon, ham, pinenuts

Cook and blend spinach. Add any quantity of cream, créme fraiche or cream cheese, strong flavoured cheese, salt, pepper and nutmeg. Pour over freshly cooked pasta. Add bacon, ham and pinenuts if you like texture.

Sassy Kelly
BRECHIN, ANGUS

Tomato and Sage – no cook sauce

SERVES AS MANY AS YOU LIKE

Several large tomatoes – skins removed and chopped
2 cloves garlic – crushed
Lots olive oil
Large handful of sage

Blend the garlic, olive oil and sage. Then add the tomatoes and blitz for a few seconds. Pour over hot pasta. That's it!

Bev Remp
INVERURIE, ABERDEENSHIRE

A Very Easy Pasta Dish

SERVES AS MANY AS YOU LIKE

Any kind of pasta
Spinach
Tomatoes – chopped (or small cherry
or plum tomotoes)
Pine nuts
Feta cheese – crumbled

Cook the pasta and at the last minute of
the cooking time add spinach leaves.
Drain well and add chopped tomatoes (or
small cherry or plum tomatoes), pine nuts
and chopped or crumbled feta cheese.
Mix well and serve.

Carol Page
CENTRE FOR NATURAL HEALTH, PERTH

Sean's Carbonara

SERVES 4

6 bacon rashers (streaky works best)
– chopped
375g spaghetti
3 egg yolks
250ml cream
30g Parmesan

Cook pasta until tender, then drain.
At the same time fry bacon until crisp.
Add hot pasta, egg yolks, cream, Parmesan
and bacon into a large pan and heat over a
low heat for 1-2 minutes.

Sean Lamont
BLAIRGOWRIE, PERTHSHIRE
SCOTLAND RUGBY INTERNATIONAL

Pasta a la Roberto

SERVES AS MANY AS YOU LIKE

Bacon
Olive oil
Garlic
Pasta
1 egg
Seasoning
2 tablespoons pesto
1 tablespoon of cream
Parmesan cheese

In a pan fry some bacon until crispy with
olive oil and garlic. Start cooking some pasta.
Meanwhile, whisk an egg, add 2
tablespoons of pesto, olive oil and the
cream. Season. Strain the pasta and
immediately pour the egg/pesto mix over
the pasta. Stir well before adding the bacon
and garlic mix.
Serve in a hot bowl with plenty of Parmesan.

Rob Teare
NEWCASTLE UNIVERSITY

Spaghetti with Tuna

SERVES 4/6

450g spaghetti
1 clove garlic – crushed
2 tablespoons olive oil
50g butter
225ml chicken stock
3 tablespoons white wine or vermouth
175g tin tuna
Freshly ground black pepper

Heat the olive oil and half the butter. Toss in the garlic for a minute. Add the stock and wine then boil until it reduces to about half a pint. Drain the tuna and add. Season with lots of ground pepper. Bring a large pan salted water to boil and cook the spaghetti. Pour over the sauce and sprinkle with chopped parsley.

Bev Remp
INVERURIE, ABERDEENSHIRE

Marsetti

SERVES 4

450g cooked mince – with onions and carrots
Pasta shells
1 tin Campbell's condensed mushroom soup
1 tin Campbell's condensed tomato soup
225g grated cheese

Mix cooked mince with unwatered soups, and boiled pasta shells. Cover with cheese, and grill until bubbling.

Dr Adrienne Swann
DALMALLY, ARGYLL

Tagliatelle with Broad Beans and Mushrooms

SERVES 4

This simple pasta is perfect for a light lunch or a casual weeknight supper. When in season, use tender baby broad beans that you can serve with their skins.

2 tablespoons olive oil, plus extra for drizzling
50g butter
2 shallots – chopped
100g chestnut mushrooms – sliced
Sea salt and freshly ground black pepper
Splash of dry white wine
300g fresh broad beans
3 tablespoons crème fraiche
500g fresh tagliatelle
2 tablespoons chopped fresh parsley
Vegetarian Parmesan, for grating

In a large saucepan, sauté the shallots in the olive oil and butter for about 5 minutes until softened but not browned. Add the sliced mushrooms, salt and pepper and cook for a few minutes until the mushrooms are golden.

Pour in a splash of white wine and cook until it has almost all evaporated. Stir in the broad beans and cook for a couple of minutes. Add the crème fraiche and check the seasoning.

Meanwhile, blanch the tagliatelle in a pot of salted boiling water for 2 minutes, then drain well. Toss with the vegetables and chopped parsley. Serve immediately with a drizzling of olive oil and a grating of Parmesan.

Gordon Ramsay
THE F WORD

Super Quick – Super Tasty Pasta

SERVES 2/4

200g penne pasta
2 chicken breasts – sliced
1 onion – sliced
6 rashers of unsmoked bacon – sliced
Mushrooms –sliced
Peas – cooked
150ml Créme fraiche

Boil the pasta and at the same time fry the chicken, bacon and onion (until it is starts to go brown). Add the mushrooms and peas to the frying pan. Finally add créme fraiche to make the sauce. (It should turn light brown, and you can add as much as you want, depending how creamy you want the sauce.) The resulting mixture can go over the pasta on a plate or mixed in once the pasta has boiled.

Gregor Townsend
SPACE CLINIC, EDINBURGH
BRITISH LION, SCOTLAND RUGBY INTERNATIONAL

Quick pasta supper

SERVES 4

500g pasta (macaroni/fusilli)
250g smoked bacon – cut into small pieces
250g mushrooms – sliced
3 or 4 tablespoons Parmesan cheese
4 eggs

Optional
Broccoli florets or 4 handfuls
sugar snap peas.

Gently boil pasta and broccoli and sugar snap peas all together in lighted salted water for 8/10 minutes. Meanwhile, in a large frying pan, lightly sauté the snipped bacon and mushrooms together till soft. Add a little butter if they start to stick to the bottom of the pan. Drain the pasta and vegetables (if added) and tip into frying pan. Gently turn ingredients together to coat the pasta. In a bowl, whisk the eggs and Parmesan cheese. Gently fold this into the pasta and cook over a low heat until the egg has set. Keep turning the pasta to ensure even cooking. When cooked, top pasta into a large bowl and serve with extra Parmesan for sprinkling.

Delicious as a meal on its own and can be served with Italian crusty bread and a salad.

Malcolm Gordon
A & E CONSULTANT, GLASGOW

Alternative Spag-Bol

SERVES 4

An all-in-one in less than an hour

1 small onion – chopped
400g mince
1 red pepper – diced
1 small courgette – diced
1 medium carrot – grated
100g mushrooms – sliced
1 can plum tomatoes or fresh if you prefer
Bay leaf
Olive oil
Black pepper
Red wine or marsala
Oregano
Parmesan cheese

Alternative Spag-Bol continued...

Fresh flat leafed parsley – chopped
Pasta of your choice

Fry onion in olive oil in a medium-sized saucepan until golden. Add mince until it falls apart. Add pepper, courgette and carrot. Stir well so it doesn't stick to the pan. After 5 minutes, add the tomatoes, mushrooms and bay leaf. Season with black pepper, red wine/marsala to your taste. Leave to cook on low 20-30 minutes. Add oregano at the end. Serve with pasta of your choice and sprinkle with parsley and Parmesan.

Dr Rachel Weldon
ISLE OF EIGG

Malloreddus Sardi

SERVES 4

Malloreddus are small pasta shells which look like large cowrie shells. If you can't find them there are similar pasta shapes which will hold a sauce well. Any good delicatessen now sells Italian pork sausages.

Malloreddus
2 to 4 Italian pork sausages
Celery
6/8 tomatoes
Glass red wine
Fennel seeds
Parsley

Sauté a few sticks of chopped celery in olive oil. Take the skin off the sausages and crumble them into the frying pan and cook.

Put the tomatoes in a bowl and add boiling water. Drain and skin the tomatoes, cut in half and discard seeds and add these to the pan. Add wine and simmer for 15/20 minutes. If wished you can add fennel seeds. Add pasta to boiling water and put a bit of the water towards end of cooking into the sauce. Drain and mix together. Garnish with parsley.

Susan Haig
BALFRON, GLASGOW

Spaghetti with Prawns and Boursin

SERVES 4

1 clove garlic – crushed
1 Boursin cheese (or similar)
Cream
Couple handfuls peeled, cooked prawns
Parsley – chopped
Spaghetti

Melt cheese and add other ingredients. Pour this sauce over cooked spaghetti and serve. Easy to double up for more and more people and perfect simplicity for after theatre supper.

Kate Nicolson
FRASERBURGH, ABERDEENSHIRE

Smoked Haddock Lasagnette

SERVES 4

Lasagne sheets
570ml boiling water in bowl
2 smoked haddock – cubed
225g leeks – sliced
50g butter
2 sprigs lemon thyme
275ml cream
2 tablespoons white wine
Zest of lemon
Seasoning
25g arrowroot with water to dissolve

Cut sheets of lasagne into 6 squares or oblongs. Place in boiling water.
   Melt the butter and leeks and gently sweat until soft 5/7 minutes. Add the haddock and thyme and warm gently for 5 minutes. Add cream to fresh saucepan with lemon zest and wine and bring to gentle simmer. Add arrowroot mixture to the sauce and check seasoning and consistency.
   Place a square of lasagne on a plate. Put 2 spoonfuls of fish mixture in the centre of the square and then cover with a little sauce. Top with a lasagne square. Do this 4 times. Add a covering of sauce to each and sprinkle with garnish of parsley, lemon zest and chives.

White Cottage Restaurant
ABOYNE, ABERDEENSHIRE

Smoked Salmon Pasta

SERVES 4

450g pasta (penne or fusilli work well with this dish)
200g smoked salmon – cut into strips
200g fine asparagus tips – chopped to 5cm pieces
200g crème fraiche
2-3 tablespoons of freshly chopped dill
Squeeze of lemon
Freshly ground pepper

Cook the pasta *al dente* (still a little crunchy). Add the asparagus tips to the boiling pasta 2 minutes before it is cooked. Drain the pasta and the asparagus and set aside. Move quickly now – heat the crème fraiche in a large pan (use your pasta pan) and add three quarters of the smoked salmon – heat through gently. Return pasta and asparagus to the pan and add half the dill and toss lightly at moderate heat for 2 minutes. Add ground pepper and lemon.
   Place in a large pasta bowl and garnish with remaining dill and put the rest of the uncooked smoked salmon around the edge of the bowl. Parma ham may be used as a substitute for smoked salmon.

Caroline Pelly
ABOYNE, ABERDEENSHIRE

Ideas for pasta and pizza sauces

Pasta does not always have to contain masses of cheese and/or cream. Simple sauces based on olive oil, garlic, lemon juice and fresh herbs and fresh greens are wonderful, good for you and really quick to make. Yoghurt works well instead of cream as long you don't cook it. Beaten eggs give a satisfying creamy sauce without the gloop. Look for the wheat-free or spelt pastas and pizza bases available and, of course, make the most of sun ripened tomatoes during the summer.

Try the following
Broccoli, toasted almonds, olive oil and rosemary.
Roasted peppers, garlic, onions with toasted pine nuts and goat's cheese.
Chickpeas, harissa, coconut milk and coriander (with roast sweet potato).
Blanched greens, frozen peas, chopped parsley, garlic and fresh ginger if you like.

Mix with your cooked pasta, return to heat and toss in a beaten egg and some yoghurt or cream until the sauce just thickens.

Jane Lorimer
LEVEN, FIFE

Wild Mushroom Risotto

SERVES 4

225g risotto rice
20g wild dried porcini mushrooms
225g mushrooms
1 onion
100ml Madeira or dry sherry
100g freshly grated Parmesan
1 clove garlic
Vegetable stock about 500ml
Good handful of chopped parsley and basil

Boil the kettle, and pour hot water into a bowl over the dried porcini to cover for half an hour or so.

Finely chop and cook the onion in a little butter over a gentle heat, cut up the mushrooms into quarters if they are small or pieces if they are large and stir into the onions. Remove dried porcini (saving the water) and add to the pan along with the other mushrooms. Stir, then add the rice and stir again until coated with the butter. Turn down the heat and add the juice from the porcini and Madeira or sherry. Let it bubble until there is not much liquid left then slowly add some vegetable stock, just to give it the consistency of thick soup. Let it bubble away and keep adding a bit of stock at a time – stirring occasionally until the rice is cooked. It is difficult to judge just how much liquid you will need before you start! When you have almost finished throw in the grated Parmesan as this gives it the creamy texture. Lastly chopped parsley and basil.

Miranda McHardy
BANCHORY, KINCARDINESHIRE

It is not polite to talk with a full mouth or an empty head

“

The racehorse bolted for about three miles over remote and rough
terrain with the rider still on board. The horse eventually lost his
footing going round a corner, throwing the rider off. He sustained
significant injuries including a tension pneumothorax (punctured
lung). With my Sandpiper Bag to hand I was able to stabilise him
sufficiently for him to survive over one hour's drive to Borders
General Hospital. He is a young married man with children, so you
can well imagine how thankful I am that I had the necessary
equipment and I would like to express my gratitude again for all the
work you are continuing to do for pre-hospital care.

GP, Hawick

fish & shellfis

h

Fish

n., *pl.* **fish** or **fishes**.
1. any of a large group of cold-blooded aquatic vertebrates having jaws, gills, and usually fins and a skin covered in scales: includes sharks and rays. **2**. the flesh of fish used as food. **3**. **a fine kettle of fish** an awkward situation; mess. **4**. **have other fish to fry** have more important activities to do.

Cajun Spiced Fillet of Salmon with Homemade Tomato Sauce

SERVES 4

4 fillets of salmon
50g of Cajun spices
Half an onion – chopped
100g tomatoes – chopped
1 teaspoon of mixed herb
2 teaspoons of brown sugar.
Half a cube of vegetable stock
Mixed salad leaves

Put 4 dessertspoons of vegetable oil in a pan and heat. Coat the fish in the spices and pan fry for roughly 4 minutes on each side.

For the tomato sauce, heat 2 dessertspoons of oil in pan. Add the onion with the tomatoes, vegetable stock and herbs then reduce by half. Add the brown sugar and blitz in food processor.

Arrange some salad leaves on plate and spoon tomato sauce in a pool. Place the salmon fillet onto tomato sauce. Drizzle salad leaves with vinaigrette and serve.

Vinaigrette
50ml olive oil
50ml orange juice
1 dessertspoon balsamic vinegar
2 teaspoons French mustard

Put all ingredients into an empty jam jar, screw on lid and shake vigorously.

Graham Seager
EDINBURGH

A Good Brown Trout

PER PERSON

Trout
Coarse grain salt
Garlic
Olive oil
Freshly ground salt and pepper
Lime juice
Mayonnaise

Carefully fillet the trout, remembering to pick out the pin bones along the centre.

Sprinkle the flesh with coarse grain salt and leave for half an hour on a flat tray tipped up at one end. Wash the fillets down with cold water and pat dry with kitchen paper. Rub a clove of garlic over the flesh and brush with olive oil.

Barbeque skin side down for fifteen minutes. Season with salt and pepper and a squeeze of lime juice and serve with mayonnaise.

This takes all the muddy water out of the trout and makes it taste like sea bass.

Johnny and Fi Warrender
RIVER STINCHAR, SOUTH AYRSHIRE

TIP...
Dieting is the penalty for exceeding the speed limit

Baked Cod with Tomato Sauce

SERVES 4

500g cod fillet
Zest of 1 lemon
50g breadcrumbs
15g coriander leaves – finely chopped
2 tablespoons olive oil

Tomato Sauce
3 tablespoons olive oil
1 onion – peeled and chopped
1 clove garlic – crushed
700g fresh tomatoes or 2 tins of chopped tomatoes
1 teaspoon sugar
1 teaspoon salt
Freshly ground black pepper

First make the sauce. Heat the oil in a heavy saucepan, add the onion and cook gently for about 5 minutes. Add the garlic and cook for another minute. Add the tomatoes and sugar. Simmer uncovered for about 30 minutes. Stir during cooking to break up the tomatoes. Serve immediately or keep in a jar in the fridge until needed.

Preheat oven to 200°C, gas mark 6. Wash the cod fillet, dry on kitchen paper and cut into 4 pieces. Place on an oiled baking tray. Mix together the breadcrumbs, coriander, lemon zest, oil and season.

Sprinkle the crumb mixture over the fish fillets and press. Bake for about 10 minutes until the fish is cooked and the topping is brown. Serve with the tomato sauce, new potatoes and green vegetables.

Maureen Wood
TARLAND, ABERDEENSHIRE

Dowalty Chilli and Garlic Prawns

SERVES 2

25g butter
2 tablespoons olive oil
4 garlic cloves
Juice of half a lemon
100ml dry white wine
Pinch dry hot red chilli pepper flakes
450g large prawns – uncooked
Freshly ground salt and pepper

Heat the butter and oil in a heavy frying pan over medium heat until melted. Add the garlic, parsley, lemon juice and wine, lower the heat and simmer for 3 minutes. Add the prawns to the frying pan and cook, stirring frequently for 5 minutes, until the prawns are just pink. Remove from the heat, place the prawns on a plate and pour over the sauce. Serve immediately with rice. This recipe can also be used for scallops.

Claire Maitland
CRATHES, KINCARDINESHIRE

TIP...
In order to reach any significant goal, you must first leave your comfort zone...

Hatton Fish

Broadly speaking 100-175g filleted fish will be more than enough for each lucky person. So ask your fish man for the equivalent with bones in.

Hatton Fish
Fish
Tin foil
Herbs
Butter and olive oil
1 lemon
Anything else you fancy…
Star anise and vermouth – both are musts

Get a good, big baking tray and put a sheet of tin foil in – much bigger than the tray. Give it a lot of olive oil and lemon juice. If you have a salmon or something with the skin on, slash the flesh a couple of times and give it a rub with pepper and salt so it goes into the cuts. If your fish has a cavity fill it up with lemon, herbs, olive oil, butter and leave plenty around the fish – including the star anise. Pour on a big glass of vermouth – Nouilly Prat is best. Just to be wicked, dot on another 25-50g butter. Don't forget plenty of sea salt and pepper. Get another piece of tin foil and make an envelope with the bottom bit, sealing it by rolling up the edges – not tight because the fish will steam and take on all the fab smells. I cook everything in the top right oven of the Aga, so go for about 200°C, gas mark 7, and give it about 20 minutes. The fish is ready when it feels slightly resistant to pressure.

   The best way to get it out is to open the packet to let the steam out and let it sit. It will finish cooking if it's not ready and not be overdone.

Jayne James-Duff
HATTON CASTLE, ABERDEENSHIRE

TIP...
If you haven't heard a good rumour by 11am start one

…and Fyvie Fish

A wild fish filleted with the skin on
Onion – chopped
Garlic – chopped
A little chopped fresh ginger
Coriander – chopped
Lime juice – PLENTY
Salt
Fresh chilli – as much as you like

All the chopped stuff goes in the middle of the fillets like a sandwich and then it is wrapped in Christmas paper (north-east lairds use tin foil for everything)
Cook as for Hatton Fish

George Forbes-Leith
FYVIE, ABERDEENSHIRE

Good and Different Orange Sauce for Salmon

SERVES 2

275ml freshly squeezed orange juice
Rind of one orange cut into julienne strips
100g unsalted butter

Put the orange juice into a small pan, add the butter and boil until it begins to thicken. Poach the julienne strips of rind separately in water until tender then add to the orange juice. Serve with baked or grilled salmon.

Enid Fenton
NEWBURGH, FIFE

Herrings Fried in Oatmeal

SERVES 2

3 fresh herrings
Half a cup of oatmeal – medium coarse
1 tablespoon of crushed junipers
Freshly ground salt and pepper
Vegetable oil for frying

Wash the herring fillets. Mix together the oatmeal, juniper berries, salt and pepper then the coat fish on both sides. Fry in very hot oil until crisp and brown. Serve immediately with bread and a tossed salad.

Dr Peter Raff
DRUMMORE, STRANRAER

Jambalaya

SERVES 8

1 head of celery
1 bulb of garlic
3 green peppers
1 bunch spring onions
1 bunch parsley
1 large tin tomatoes
1 pint chicken stock
1 cup basmati rice
1 teaspoon sugar
1 teaspoon thyme
1 teaspoon oregano
3 bay leaves
1 tablespoon creole seasoning (if available)
Half a cup of sliced chorizo sausage
Selection of seafood (mussels, shelled prawns, squid)
Tabasco to taste
Chopped coriander

Chop the vegetables, garlic and herbs. Sauté the celery, green peppers, garlic and spring onions in olive oil until soft. Add the parsley and cook for a further minute. Add the spices, tomatoes, sugar and chicken stock. Bring to the boil and add the rice. Stir occasionally until the rice has absorbed most of the liquid. Season with black pepper. Add the chorizo. If you want it spicy add a few drops of Tabasco to taste. Add the fish and seafood and put in a large ovenproof dish and cover with foil. Bake for about fifteen minutes until the seafood is cooked through. Sprinkle with chopped coriander and serve with garlic bread and a tossed salad.

Beth Nicholson
KILNINVER, ARGYLL

Fish, to taste right, must swim three times – in water, in butter and in wine

Polish proverb

Kedgeree

SERVES 4

4 haddock fillets
4 eggs
200g brown organic rice
Butter

Butter a medium-sized oven proof dish. Hard boil the eggs. Put the rice into a large saucepan and bring to the boil. While the rice is cooking put the fish into a steamer or colander with a lid on and put on top of a pan of boiling water. By the time the rice is cooked the fish will be ready.

Assemble the kedgeree in an oven proof dish. Layer the rice, fish, chopped up eggs, and season each layer with salt and pepper and knobs of butter. Finish off with a final knob or two of butter. Put on the lid, or cover with foil, put in a medium oven and heat gently. This will sit for a day in the fridge before being heated up again. Serve a fresh green salad and some crunchy bread.

Rosamund Pilcher
LONGFORGAN, PERTHSHIRE

Monkfish with Ginger and Lime

SERVES 4

700g monkfish
Juice of 2 limes
4cm ginger – sliced
4 cloves garlic – chopped
Olive oil
Freshly ground salt and pepper

Chop the monkfish into 3cm cubes. Mix in a large bowl with the other ingredients. Add enough olive oil to coat the fish well and season. Cover and leave in the fridge for at least 2 hours.

Remove the fish from its marinade and barbeque for a few minutes on each side until cooked through or fry in a little olive oil.

Sera Irvine
TARLAND, ABERDEENSHIRE

Moroccan Fish Dish

SERVES 4

1 teaspoon ground ginger
1 teaspoon ground coriander
1 teaspoon ground cinnamon
Quarter teaspoon ground cardamon
225g tomatoes – tinned or fresh
500g fresh haddock
1 lemon
Vegetable oil
Freshly ground salt and pepper

Heat the oil in a frying pan and sauté the tomatoes and spices for fifteen minutes on a medium heat taking care not to burn the mixture.

Meanwhile, put the haddock into an ovenproof dish and squeeze lemon juice over. Season with salt and pepper. Pour the tomatoes on top of the haddock and place in a very hot oven for ten minutes. Serve with rice or tabouleh.

Georgie Sampson
FORFAR, ANGUS

Orange and Haddock Bake

SERVES 4

700g haddock fillets
Juice of 3 oranges
1 tablespoon chopped parsley
25g butter
150g Cheddar cheese
225g tomatoes
75g breadcrumbs

Preheat the oven to 180°C, gas mark 4. Grease an ovenproof dish. Place the haddock fillets in the dish, cover with orange juice, parsley and tomato. Sprinkle with grated cheese and breadcrumbs dotted with butter. Cover with foil and bake for 20 minutes. Finish under grill.

Caroline Southesk
KINNAIRD, ANGUS

Salmon Belnagarrow

SERVES 4

I make this a lot and devised it many years ago in my mother's kitchen.

4 salmon fillets
50g mushrooms – finely chopped
2 tablespoon sunflower oil
1 tablespoon lemon juice
Quarter teaspoon grated lemon rind
1 tablespoon coarse grain mustard
1 spring onion or chives
Few sprigs of parsley – chopped
Freshly ground salt and pepper

Heat the grill until very hot. In a bowl mix the oil, lemon juice and rind, mustard, mushrooms and breadcrumbs. Snip in the spring onions or chives and most of the parsley. Season and mix well. Grill the fillets, skin side up for one or two minutes. Turn the fish over. Spread the mixture over the fleshy side of the fillets. Grill until the crust is firm and the fish is cooked. Sprinkle over the remaining parsley and serve with new potatoes and fresh garden vegetables.

Jim and Jean Royan
JIM IS CHAIRMAN NHS GRAMPIAN
PLUSCARDEN, MORAYSHIRE

Salmon with Crunchy Mustard

PER PERSON

Salmon or cod
Butter
Fine breadcrumbs
Coarse grain mustard – for salmon or
Parsley, chopped thyme, marjoram – for cod

Preheat oven to 220°C, gas mark 7. Use one piece of salmon or cod steak per person. Brush the fish with butter and put in an buttered ovenproof dish without the fish pieces touching. Grind some black pepper over them. **For salmon** – mix the breadcrumbs with the mustard; **for cod** – mix the breadcrumbs with the herbs. Pat a layer on top of the fish. Dot on any left over butter. Cook for 8 to 12 minutes.

Liz Vyvyan
LONDON

Salmon with Vegetables

SERVES 2

2 salmon steaks
2 leeks – sliced
2 carrots – sliced
2 courgettes – sliced
1 clove garlic – chopped
Salt and pepper
15g butter
1 tablespoon olive oil

In a frying pan melt the butter and olive oil together. Seal the salmon on both sides. Add the vegetables and season.
Put a lid on the pan and cook gently for fifteen minutes.

Dr. Lizzie Finlayson
ABOYNE, ABERDEENSHIRE

Sea Bass fillets with Tomato and Olive Oil

SERVES 4

4 fillets sea bass
1 tin chopped tomatoes
6 tablespoons olive oil
2 cloves garlic – crushed
2 tablespoons parsley – finely chopped
1 fresh chilli – finely chopped
Half glass white wine
Freshly ground salt and pepper

Heat the oil in a wide shallow pan adding the garlic, parsley and chilli. Cook for two minutes then add the tomatoes and cook for a further two minutes. Add the wine, raise the heat and let it bubble for two minutes.

Season. Lower the heat and lay the sea bass fillets, skin side up, in the pan. Cover and cook for five minutes. Serve the fillets, skin down, pour the sauce over.

Claire Maitland
CRATHES, KINCARDINESHIRE

Seafood Gratin

PER PERSON

2 red onions - chopped
50g butter
Prawns and any other seafood
Sweet chilli dipping sauce
Créme fraiche
Gruyére cheese

Sauté the onions in the butter over a medium heat until soft. Line the bottom of an ovenproof dish with the cooked onions. Cover the onions with prawns and any other seafood. Pour sweet chilli dipping sauce over the fish and on that pour a layer of crème fraiche. Sprinkle with grated Gruyére cheese. Put under grill until brown and bubbling. Serve immediately.

Clare Reid Scott
LONDON

Seared Salmon on a bed of Stir Fried Vegetables in Oyster Sauce

SERVES 4

4 x 100g salmon fillets
Malden sea salt
1 tablespoon vegetable oil
Mixture of vegetables – finely chopped
Beansprouts
Sesame oil
Oyster sauce

Preheat oven 180°C, gas mark 4. Sprinkle the skin of the salmon with Maldon salt. Take a thick frying pan and heat the oil. When it begins to smoke put in the salmon, skin side down and cook on a high flame until skin is coloured and crispy. Turn the salmon over and transfer to hot oven until just cooked for about four minutes.

Stir fry a mix of vegetables and beansprouts in sesame oil and add the oyster sauce. Arrange the vegetables on a plate and put the salmon on top. Decorate with lemon and herbs.

Bob Ovington
PITTODRIE HOUSE HOTEL, ABERDEENSHIRE

Simon's Simple Seafood

SERVES 4

Mixture of fish (prawns, squid, cod, haddock, mussels etc.)
Juice of 1 lemon
Spring onions – chopped
Crème fraiche
Oil for frying

Heat a little oil in a pan and throw in the seafood and some spring onions. Cook briefly – overcooking will ruin it. Sprinkle half the lemon juice on and add salt and pepper. Stir in crème fraiche. Add the rest of the lemon juice and stir again. Serve with rice.

Simon Dickson
DOUNE, PERTHSHIRE

Smoked Haddock Chowder

SERVES 4

4 pieces undyed smoked haddock
250ml low fat crème fraiche
500ml milk
2 small leeks – sliced
8 small waxy potatoes boiled
Butter
Parsley

Gently fry the leeks in butter until wilted, add the cut up haddock, (doesn't matter if its not undyed) and cook for a minute. Pour in the milk and low fat crème fraiche. Heat through and cook gently for another minute, then add the cut up cooked potatoes. You can really put as many of these in as you like to pad it out if an extra person arrives suddenly.

Chuck in a handful of chopped parsley at the end. Serve in big soup bowls with some warm bread. This is a wonderful instant lunchtime or supper dish.

Miranda McHardy
BANCHORY, KINCARDINESHIRE

Smoked Haddock with Coconut and Courgette

SERVES 4

4 fillets undyed smoked haddock
2 small organic courgettes
1 tin coconut milk – strained
Chopped coriander

Preheat oven to 200°C, gas mark 7. Grate the courgette and set aside. Empty the coconut milk through a strainer and keep the liquid to drink or put in a soup. Mix the courgette, coconut cream, coriander and a twist of black pepper. Lay the fish on your left palm, take a small heap of the mixture and mould it onto tail half of the fillet, fold the top over and lay in a baking dish. Bake in the hot oven for 8-10 minutes. Garnish with coriander or snipped chives. Serve with a dark green salad or sautéd pak choi and some new potatoes – or try quinoa or wild rice with tomato paste stirred through.

Jane Lorimer
LEVEN, FIFE

Another Kedgeree...

SERVES 2 GENEROUSLY

2 pieces smoked haddock – dyed or undyed
2 eggs
1 onion – finely chopped
1 clove garlic – chopped
2 heaped tablespoons sultanas
4 tablespoons Basmati rice
Large knob of butter – the more the better!
1 teaspoon curry powder
Freshly ground salt and pepper
Large handful prawns
Fresh parsley
Mango chutney to serve

Boil the eggs until hard. Cool them in cold water, peel and put aside.
    Put the fish into a flattish dish and pour over a measured pint of boiling water. Leave the fish to cook like this.
    Fry the onions in butter over a low heat. Don't rush this bit and don't burn the onion – it should be sticky and translucent. Now add the garlic and fry for another minute. Stir in the curry powder, sultanas and rice. Again – don't let it burn. Heat through until the spices have infused into the rice. Now take the water from the fish and pour over the rice mixture keeping the fish warm – you will have a soupy, rice substance which doesn't look that appetising! Bubble until it's reduced and the rice is cooked – you shouldn't have to add anymore water. Flake the fish – which should be just cooked. Add to the rice and stir carefully. Throw in the prawns and parsley and gently heat. Serve with quartered boiled eggs and mango chutney.

Fiona Hill
GLASS, ABERDEENSHIRE

"

Lorry off road in field, rain like only west of Scotland can produce. Some comfort provided by protective jacket and Sandpiper equipment in bag. I did have to utilise one non standard item that Sandpiper does not provide, namely a strapping young farmer to carry the bag over rough ground!

GP, Castle Douglas

chicken & game

Chicken *n*. **1**. a domestic fowl bred for its flesh or eggs, esp. a young one. **2**. the flesh of such a bird used for food. **3**. *Slang*. a cowardly person. **4**. *Slang*. a young inexperienced person. **5**. *Informal*. any of various, often dangerous, games or challenges in which the object is to make one's opponent lose his nerve. **6**. **no spring chicken** *Slang*. no longer young ie 'she's no...' **7**. **chicken feed** *Slang*. a trifling amount of money.

Game *n*. **1**. wild animals, including birds and fish, hunted for sport, food or profit. **2**. the flesh of such animals used as food. **3**. an object of pursuit; quarry; prey (esp. in the phrase **fair game**) **4**. **game bird** *Slang*. a woman who's up for a good time.

Chicken Tikka Masala

SERVES 4

450g chicken breast – cubed
2 tablespoons Sharwood's Tikka seasoning
1 tablespoon oil
205ml milk
1 can Campbell's condensed tomato soup

Coat chicken in tikka seasoning. Heat oil. Fry chicken for 5 minutes. Stir in soup and milk. Simmer 25 minutes or until chicken is cooked. Serve with rice and naan bread. Can add yoghurt or cream if liked.

Val Rahtz
ECHT, ABERDEENSHIRE

Chicken and Tomato Casserole

PER PERSON

2 chicken thighs
6/8 baby potatoes
Juice of half a lemon
2 tablespoons olive oil
1 tablespoon balsamic vinegar
6 small plum tomatoes
1 tablespoon dark brown sugar
Quarter/half glass white wine

Preheat oven to 190°C, gas mark 5. Put chicken thighs in large dish skin up. Cut baby potatoes in half and scatter between chicken pieces. Pour juice of lemon over chicken and sprinkle with olive oil and balsamic vinegar. Put into preheated oven for 40 minutes. In separate bowl put plum tomatoes (6 per person) cut in half lengthways and sprinkle with sugar. Stir together. Take chicken out of the oven after 20 minutes and scatter tomatoes between chicken pieces – do not stir in. Add quarter to half glass of white wine per person. Put back into oven for another 20/30 minutes until chicken skins are nice and crispy.

Liz Vyvyan
LONDON

Cadzow Cajun Chicken

SERVES 4

4 chicken breasts
Cajun spice – amount depends on how hot you like it.
Lime juice
Coriander – either fresh or out of a tube!
Olive oil – enough to moisten chicken breasts.
Freshly ground salt and pepper

Preheat oven to 200°C, gas mark 6. Score breasts with sharp knife, this allows the spices to permeate. Add all the ingredients and rub into the scores. This can be done a few hours before cooking. Bung onto a baking tray and put in the oven for 15 minutes. Then put under the grill for a further 5 minutes to brown.
    This is also delicious cooked on a barbecue, except you lose the lovely juices. Serve with a yummy salad, new potatoes and chives

Tooti Cadzow
ISLE OF LUING, ARGYLL

Marquess Chicken

SERVES 2

Two chicken breasts
– boneless and skinless
Olive oil
Linghams sweet chilli sauce
Garlic – crushed
Soy sauce
Fresh coriander
Lemon juice
A little salt (as soy is salty)
Black pepper

Slice chicken breasts along their length into medium thickness and place in a bowl. Pour over olive oil to nearly cover and add all the other ingredients in measure to suit yourself and roughly chopped coriander. Stir well together and allow to marinate for a couple of hours.

Fry in a frying pan and use a large measure of the marinade to do so until it has almost gone dry and eat as soon as ready with some boiled and buttered broccoli.

Alexander Aberdeen
HADDO, ABERDEENSHIRE

Thai Chicken

SERVES 6

6 chicken breasts, skin on
– or chicken thighs
1 tin coconut milk
1 bunch coriander
1-2 birds eye chillies
– deseeded and chopped
3-4 cloves garlic
2 limes, rind and juice
3 tablespoons soy sauce
2cm piece of fresh ginger grated
2 level tablespoons caster sugar

Preheat oven to 200°C, gas mark 6. Mix all the ingredients together and marinade the chicken for a few hours or overnight in the fridge. Remove from fridge an hour or so before cooking. Bake in oven for 40-45 minutes until chicken is cooked through and the skin is golden.

Louisa Leader
GLENCARSE, PERTHSHIRE

TIP...
If you think you are going to blow everyone's head off with the heat from chilli, add another spoonful of sugar. If you do have your head blown off by someone else's curry, eat a teaspoon of sugar to take away the sweating and pain! DON'T just drink more liquid.

Cockerel with Veggies and Wine

SERVES 6

STAGE 1 Next time you hear a neighbour complaining they have too many cockerels and need to get rid of some... accept – on condition that you can have a hen as well. Generally people give birds away in the autumn just before the hen stops laying and the cockerel will be less vigorous with his crowing.

STAGE 2 Build an enclosure and chicken hutch – an amusing afternoon's entertainment that may involve borrowing interesting stone moving equipment from friends and neighbours. Tramp picker, long handles spade, 2 metre metal bar... dumper. The birds will fly out of the enclosure as soon as the clipped wings grow, but it makes you feel better to have protected them from foxes.

STAGE 3 Spring – early summer
Hopefully hennie is laying an egg a day and the pair potter about digging up small delicate plants and eating slugs.
The cockerel may or may not stay in the coop at night, so roosting in the tree under your bedroom window will be waking you earlier and earlier in the morning. This lack of sleep and resulting exasperation is essential for stage four.

STAGE 4 Catch and kill the cockerel
People who tell you how easy it is to kill a bird probably read it in a book. In my experience people who have actually done it keep very quiet about the event. You will find a way, because the b….y thing has been keeping you awake at night for the last three weeks. But if you have a friendly butcher you could take it in a box for him to dispatch, pluck and gut... if you can catch it.

STAGE 5 Pluck and gut
I have taken to skinning the bird with feathers on; it saves having feathers flying about. Same principle as skinning a rabbit, and there are many ways to do that. Best keep children away from the gutting bit, as the smell can be off putting.

STAGE 6 Make into a stew with lots of veggies and wine... (you all know how to do that) – and cook low and slow – about 7 hours. The flavour of the meat is superb. You will probably never eat a supermarket chicken again!

Susie Hunt
KEMNAY, ABERDEENSHIRE

Alice's Chicken

SERVES 6

6 chicken breasts
Pot double cream
Half jar sundried tomatoes – chopped up
1 clove garlic
Generous handful chopped up basil
Squeeze lemon
Half a glass of dry white wine

Cut chicken breasts into strips, fry them in a little olive oil, add the pot of double cream, then add the sun dried tomatoes, garlic, salt, pepper, basil, lemon and wine. Simmer and serve with mini roast potatoes or rice and greens of your choice.

Alice Lane
OXFORD BROOKES UNIVERSITY

Barbecue Chicken Thighs

SERVES 4

6/8 chicken thighs
2 tablespoons soy sauce
2 tablespoons Worcestershire sauce
2 tablespoons honey
2 tablespoons tomato sauce
2 teaspoons Dijon mustard

Preheat oven to 200°C, gas mark 6. Mix the above, then pour over chicken thighs (with some skin left on). Cook in preheated oven for 40 minutes.

Fi Strang-Steel
BANCHORY, KINCARDINESHIRE

Stir Fried Chicken with Lime and Coconut

SERVES 4

4 traditional chicken breasts – skinless and boneless
Grated zest and juice of 2 limes
300ml tinned coconut milk
2 dessertspoons olive oil
1 green chilli – deseeded and finely chopped
2 dessertspoons Thai fish sauce
6 heaped tablespoons fresh coriander leaves
6 spring onions cut into 1 inch (2.5cm) shreds, including green parts

You will also need a frying pan or a wok.

First of all chop the chicken into bite-sized pieces and place them in a bowl with the lime juice and zest and leave them to marinate for about an hour. Prepare the remaining ingredients. When you're ready to cook the chicken, heat the oil in the pan or wok over a high heat, add the chicken pieces and stir-fry for 3-4 minutes, until they're golden. Then add the chilli. Stir-fry for 1 more minute and add the coconut milk, fish sauce and half the coriander and spring onions. Cook for another 1-2 minutes, then serve with wild/basmati rice with the remaining coriander and spring onions sprinkled over.

Julia Leslie-Melville
MILNATHORT, FIFE

Thai Green Curry

SERVES 4

4 chicken breasts
Green curry paste
Coconut milk (tinned is usually easier)
1 tablespoon brown sugar
Lime juice

Bring all these ingredients to the boil then throw in your chicken breasts. Simmer in a pan for 15-20 minutes until the chicken is cooked through.

You can add red peppers and baby corn if you like and the final touch is a wee bit of coriander on top. Nice and easy and very tasty.

Chris Paterson
GALASHIELS
SCOTLAND RUGBY CAPTAIN

...a variation

5 large chicken/pheasant breasts
2 tablespoons of green Thai curry paste
400ml (one can) coconut milk
3 bay leaves
1 tablespoon of brown sugar
Splash of Thai fish sauce
Aubergine if desired

Heat olive oil in pan or wok, add paste and sugar and mix on fairly high heat add diced chicken breasts and sear. Reduce heat and add coconut milk, bay leaves and fish sauce. Cook on low heat 25-30mins (add aubergine half way through). Serve with rice.

Ed Clerk
PENICUIK, MIDLOTHIAN

Chicken and Olive Casserole

SERVES 6

It's important to get good pesto and olives for this.

2 tablespoons oil
12 chicken thighs
1 clove garlic – crushed
2 x 400g tins chopped tomatoes
2 tablespoons basil pesto
100g black pitted olives
Salt and pepper
Basil to garnish

Preheat oven to 350°C, gas mark 4.
Heat oil in large pan and brown chicken joints. Remove and put in casserole.
Put tomatoes, garlic, pesto and olives in a pan and heat – scraping base of pan to get chicken bits. Bring to the boil and season.
Pour over chicken and bake for 30 minutes.
Remove from the oven and garnish with fresh basil. Serve with couscous.

Vicks Drysdale
CUPAR, FIFE

Chicken Crumble

SERVES 6/8

455g cooked chicken
115g each of butter, flour and grated cheese
225g mushrooms – lightly fried
2 x 315g tin condensed mushroom soup
1 x 200 ml carton crème fraiche

Preheat oven to 200C, gas mark 6.

Put cooked chicken and mushrooms in ovenproof dish. Mix mushroom soup and crème fraiche together and pour over chicken. Mix together the butter and flour until crumbly and mix in the grated cheese. Put the mixture on top of the chicken and bake for 20 minutes.

Victoria Willis
FETTERCAIRN, KINCARDINESHIRE

Sheriff's Chicken

SERVES 4

Easy peasy

2 cloves garlic
1 (or more) birds eye chilli
Thumb's length of ginger – chopped
4 chicken breasts – sliced into flaps
2 tablespoons sugar
Oyster sauce
String beans – shaped into thumb lengths

Mix the sugar with the chicken and leave to sit whilst getting on with the rest.
  Lightly blanch the string beans and drain. Leave to the side. Finely chop the garlic and chilli together. Slice the ginger into matchsticks. Fry in a little vegetable oil until fragrant and getting a bit golden (not burning). When ready, add the sugary chicken and cook altogether. Add a glug of oyster sauce. Add the blanched beans and then keep adding as much sauce as you want. Serve with steamed rice.

Sondra Sheriff
EDINBURGH UNIVERSITY

Lucy's Wine and Thyme Chicken

SERVES 4

4 Chicken breasts, legs or 8 thighs – skin on
6 whole garlic cloves
1 big glass of dry white wine
Juice of 1 lemon
Dessertspoon of fresh (or dried) thyme
Freshly ground salt and pepper

Heat a little oil in a heavy saucepan with lid. Add the chicken skin side down first and brown the meat all over. (Don't add too much meat at a time or you will steam and not brown it). Remove to a plate then do the next batch. Leave the heat turned up and put all the chicken back in the saucepan, season with black pepper and a little salt, add the whole garlic cloves (which you can bash lightly first under the flat side of a knife to leave whole but a bit open to let the flavour out). Pour in the white wine (stand back, it will sizzle like mad!), add the thyme and juice of the lemon. The chicken should be almost but not quite covered by the liquid, if it isn't, add a bit of boiling water or chicken stock.
  Turn the heat right down to just simmering, put the lid on and leave to simmer very gently for around 20 minutes. You can leave it for longer if you like but check to see the liquid is still there. Check the chicken is cooked before serving.
  This goes well with brown basmati rice (if using brown rice, start cooking it more-or-less the same time as the chicken as it takes around 20 - 25 minutes) and broccoli or green salad.

Lucy Pelham Burn
BATTERSEA, LONDON

Chicken Curry

SERVES 2

This curry is good served with bought naan bread, cucumber raita, sliced banana, mango chutney and carrot salad.

2 dessertspoons cooking oil
2 chicken breasts
1 onion
1 or 2 cloves of garlic
2 teaspoons curry powder
1 chicken stock cube
1 small tin tomatoes
125gm long grain or basmati rice

Chop onion and crush or chop garlic. Heat the oil in a saucepan and add onions and garlic and cook until soft. Take off heat, cut the chicken into bite size pieces. Return pan to the heat, add the chicken and stir until flesh changes colour. Add curry powder stir and cook over a gentle heat. Add tinned tomatoes and chicken stock cube dissolved in a little water. Add a little more water if the curry seems a bit dry. Bring to the boil, lower the heat and simmer for approximately 40 minutes. (You could also add mushrooms, peppers any colour, courgettes, raisins or mango chutney at the same time as the tinned tomatoes).

Cucumber Raita (to accompany curry)
Quarter cucumber
1 small tub natural yoghurt
Half green chilli – finely chopped or small
Pinch of chilli powder
Quarter teaspoon salt
Quarter teaspoon cumin powder
Pinch red paprika

Peel cucumber and course grate or very

finely chop. Put yoghurt in bowl. Add salt, cumin powder and chilli and mix thoroughly. Add cucumber. Put in serving bowl and sprinkle with a bit of paprika Refrigerate until ready to eat

Carrot Salad
This sounds boring but I cannot tell you how good it is – and it's cheap and looks so good on the table for everyone to help themselves

225g carrots
Quarter teaspoon salt
Quarter teaspoon black mustard seeds
Half teaspoon lemon juice
1 tablespoon vegetable oil

Trim and peel carrots and then grate OR finely chop them into long thin strips. Put oil and mustard seeds in a pan over medium heat and cover with a lid (essential as they pop everywhere). When seeds are roasted (stopped popping) add the carrots, salt and lemon juice. Add 1 green chilli cut into very fine long strips if you like a hot salad.

Bananas and coconut
Sliced bananas
Dessicated coconut
Lemon juice

Mix together

Carina McGuinness
EAST LINTON, EAST LOTHIAN

Chicken Kebabs

SERVES 4

1 organic chicken, jointed. Separate each drumstick into two portions and cut the breast meat into 3.5cm chunks.
(or buy chicken breasts and joints)
1 large carton of organic plain unsweetened yoghurt
1 pack of wooden skewers
1 teaspoon saffron soaked in
2 tablespoon hot water
Juice of 2 limes
2 tbsp olive oil
2 large onions – finely sliced
2 tbsp plain yoghurt
1 teaspoon salt
Freshly ground black pepper

In a large bowl, combine all the ingredients, and marinade for 6 to 48 hours.
    Soak the skewers for half an hour, and then chill in the fridge or freezer.
    About 20 minutes before cooking, light the barbecue and let it burn until the coals are glowing. Spear the chicken pieces on the chilled skewers, and when the barbecue is ready, grill them for about 15 minutes, turning regularly. Baste the chicken with the marinade, butter or lime juice if required.
    The chicken is done when the juice that runs out is not pink. Serve with barbecued tomatoes, basil and pitta bread.

Dr Kate Dawson
SOUTH UIST, BENBECULA

Quick Chicken Supper Dish

SERVES 2

4 rashers smoked bacon – chopped
2 chicken breasts
1 onion
12 mushrooms
1 teaspoon mixed herbs
250ml double cream

Fry the chopped bacon and onion until the bacon is crisp. Add the diced chicken and fry until brown and thoroughly cooked through. Add the mushrooms and continue to stir until cooked. Add salt and pepper to taste, add the herbs and pour over the cream. Stir through and when warm serve with a baked potato, rice or pasta and a green salad.

Margaret Goude
FETTES COLLEGE, EDINBURGH

Mango Chicken with Cashew Nuts

SERVES 8

This is a welcome change from coronation chicken!

1 large or 2 small mangos
5 heaped tablespoons mayonnaise
200g yoghurt (plain or greek)
2 teaspoon curry powder
2 heaped tablespoons mango chutney
8 ready cooked chicken breasts
100g roast cashew nuts
Lettuce or chicory
Freshly ground salt and Pepper

Mango chicken with cashew nuts continued...

Peel mango, cut flesh off each side of the stone and cut into strips for decoration. Cut off remaining mango around the stone and blend in a food processor with mayonnaise, yoghurt, curry powder, mango chutney, salt and pepper. Remove skin from chicken breasts and cut into bite size pieces, you can prepare up to this point the day before.

Mix mango mayonnaise with chicken and half cashew nuts, arrange lettuce around large serving dish. Put mango chicken in the middle and decorate with remaining nuts and mango strips.

(It is OK to prepare mango in advance as long as it is covered in cling film and placed in fridge).

Lorna McGuire
ST CYRUS, ANGUS

Harrison's Chicken and Parmesan

SERVES AS MANY AS YOU LIKE

Bits of chicken (works well with thighs, breasts and drumsticks) – amount dependent on how many you need to feed
Four tablespoons of olive oil
Some potatoes – amount dependent on how many you need to feed
Juice of a lemon and the roughly chopped zest of half of it
Half a bottle of white wine
Some chicken stock
A big hunk of Parmesan grated
5 or so bay leaves

Preheat oven to 180C, gas mark 4. Brown the chicken in the oil and then add everything, covering it all with the grated Parmesan. Put into preheated oven, leave to cook until there's not much liquid left (up to a couple of hours) and everything is congealing.

Serve with crusty bread and salad.

Robert and Helen Harrison
FETTES COLLEGE, EDINBURGH

Chicken with Roasted Root Vegetables

SERVES 4

1 whole chicken – jointed
or 1 chicken breast per person

Marinated for at least 1 hour (preferably overnight) in:
50ml Olive oil
1 tablespoon Paprika
2 crushed cloves of Garlic
Parsley/Thyme/Rosemary

Vegetables:
carrots/potatoes/parsnips/
beetroot/celeriac/turnip/
artichokes/onions

Preheat oven to 180°C, gas mark 4. Cut vegetables into roughly equal bits and drizzle with oil and seasoning. Place all ingredients in a large dish cook for around 45 minutes to 1 hour, turning occasionally.

Dr Lizzie Finlayson
ABOYNE, ABERDEENSHIRE

Mediterranean Chicken

SERVES 4

This dish is best served with roasted sweet potatoes.

4 large skinless boneless chicken breasts
250g cherry tomatoes on the vine
4 tablespoons capers – rinsed
4 tablespoons olive oil
2 tablespoons balsamic vinegar
12 pitted black olives

Preheat oven to 190°C, gas mark 5.
Place chicken and tomatoes in a roasting tin. Season with plenty of black pepper, scatter over the capers, then add the olive oil and vinegar. Put in oven for 20 minutes. Add olives to the tin and cook for another 5 minutes until chicken cooked through.

Jo Braithwaite
DOUNE, PERTHSHIRE

Jubilee Chicken

SERVES 8/10

10 smoked chicken breasts (or cooked plain chicken breasts, skin removed)
50g chopped red onion
25g chopped shallots
1 tablespoon olive oil
357ml chicken velouté (thick chicken stock)
150ml milk – warm and infused with thyme
2 limes
150ml crème fraîche
10g grated ginger root
25g chopped flat leaf parsley

Chop the chicken. In a frying pan, cook the onion and shallot in the olive oil until soft but not brown. Add the milk and reduce. Add the chicken velouté, juice of the limes and ginger and cook for five minutes or until it coats the back of a spoon (ie it is quite thick). Strain into a bowl and cool.
    Once cool, add the crème fraîche. Combine with the chicken pieces. Garnish with the zest of the limes and the parsley.
    Serve with a cold pasta or rice salad.

Chef to the Royal Household

Chicken Fillets and Sun Dried Tomatoes

SERVES 4

This would also work well with pheasant breasts

4 chicken breasts
I packet smoked pancetta or bacon
6 dry sun dried tomatoes cut into slivers
2 tablespoons olive oil
110g butter

Slice chicken breasts lengthwise into 3 or 4 flat pieces. Push slivers of tomato into the chicken pieces. Lay out a slice of pancetta and roll tightly around chicken pieces Heat oil and butter in a large frying pan until smoking, place rolls into the pan. By the time they are all in the first one will be ready for turning. Turn frequently for 3-5 minutes.

Richmond Haddow
ALYTH, PERTHSHIRE

Zeph's Malawi Chicken BBQ

SERVES 4

1 chicken cut up or the equivalent in pieces
2 large chopped onions
1 cup chopped green peppers
1 cup tomato sauce
1 cup stock
2 tablespoons brown sugar
2 tablespoons Worcestershire sauce
1 tablespoons tomato chutney

Preheat oven to 180°C, gas mark 4.
Season and fry chicken until golden brown.
Remove from pan and transfer to an
ovenproof casserole. Add rest of ingredients
to pan and cook the sauce for a bit then
pour over the chicken. Cook in preheated
oven for one to one and a half hours.

Muriel Bain
ABERDEEN

Chicken Gratin

SERVES 4

1 tablespoons olive oil
6 chicken thighs (boned & skinned) - cut
into pieces
100g chestnut mushrooms - sliced
2 cloves of garlic - chopped (or just press it)
4 rashers of pancetta - chopped (or for
ease use cubetti di pancetta)
300ml double cream
75g Gruyére cheese - grated
2 tablespoons grated Parmesan
Handful fresh breadcrumbs (on no account
use that yellow stuff)

Preheat oven to 200°C, gas mark 6.
Fry pancetta and garlic, add chicken for a
few minutes to just start cooking. Add
mushrooms for a further few minutes - all
partly cooked – add cream and seasoning.
Turn into an oven dish, top with cheesy
breadcrumbs. Cook in preheated oven for 20
minutes. Can prepare ahead and cook the
next day.

Lisa Bain
ABERDEEN

Partridge with Strathdon Blue Cheese

SERVES 4

4 partridges
4 walnut size pieces of Strathdon blue
cheese
300ml partridge (or pheasant) stock
300ml cider
2 tablepsoons olive oil
Freshly ground salt and pepper

Preheat the oven to 190 °C, gas mark 5.
Put a piece of blue cheese inside each
partridge. Heat the oil in the casserole.
Brown the partridges all over and cover.
Place the casserole in the oven for half an
hour. Remove and check that the juices run
clear. Put the partridges on a warming plate.
Deglaze the casserole dish with the stock
and cider. Reduce the liquid to half. Remove
the fat and season to taste.
    Serve partridges whole.

Ronald Munro-Ferguson
NOVAR, ROSS-SHIRE

V's Roast Chicken

SERVES 4

8 chicken thighs (organic of course!) or
mixture of thighs and drumsticks
1 lemon plus juice of extra half lemon
1 medium onion – thinly sliced
6 large garlic cloves – peeled and bashed
with the flat of a knife
3/4 bushy sprigs fresh rosemary
– roughly torn
2 tablespoons olive oil
Sea salt and freshly ground pepper

Preheat oven to 190°C, gas mark 5.
Place chicken in a large bowl. Cut lemon
into quarters lengthways then cut each
quarter into thin slices widthways, skin and
all. Add lemon to the chicken, together with
sliced onion, bashed garlic cloves, rosemary,
olive oil and season generously.
   Mix everything together and leave to
marinate for anything up to 24 hours.
 Place everything into a heavy roasting pan,
skin side up, spread out if possible, with all
the marinade. Squeeze over the extra lemon
juice and bake for about 40 minutes, basting
from time to time. If it needs a little extra
browning turn the oven up for the last ten
minutes.
   Good served either hot or at room
temperature.

V Reid
DOUNE, PERTHSHIRE

Mugdrum BBQ Chicken

SERVES 4

4 chicken breasts
1 medium carton of plain yoghurt
I small onion – finely chopped
1 tablespoon vinegar
1 tablespoon lemon juice
1 tablespoon Worcestershire sauce
1 teaspoon crushed cardamom pods
1 teasooon cumin
Half a teaspoon ginger
1 tablespoon curry powder
1 chilli – chopped

Mix all the ingredients in large bowl. Pour
over the chicken, cover and leave in fridge
overnight. Drain, then barbecue or grill.

Enid Fenton
NEWBURGH, FIFE

Sunday Chicken

SERVES 4

1 small tin Campbell's chicken soup
4 chicken breasts
2 teaspoons curry powder
1 onion – chopped
1 eating apple – chopped
1 tablespoon butter
100ml double cream
100g mushrooms

Preheat oven to 180°C, gas mark 6.
Cook apple, onions and mushrooms in
butter. Add curry powder, salt and pepper.
In bowl combine the soup and cream then
mix with the vegetable mixture.

Sunday chicken continued...

Place the sauce in a flat oven dish and lay chicken on top, sprinkle with paprika.
Do not cover. Roast for 1 and a half hours.

Linda Harper
G-MED – ABERDEEN

Greenwood's Puff Pastry

PER PERSON

1 chicken breast
Mushrooms – chopped
Garlic – chopped
Puff pastry
1 egg

Preheat oven to 180°C, gas mark 4.
Fry the mushrooms and garlic in a pan.
Slice chicken breasts and stuff with the cooked mushrooms and if necessary, skewer them to hold them together.
Cook for 15 minutes. Remove from the oven.
   Roll out the pastry on a floured board – not too thin. Cut it into 2.5cm strips and wrap about four pieces around each breast.
Glaze with beaten egg and return to the oven until golden brown.
Serve with curly kale and new potatoes.

Johnnie Greenwood
NEWCASTLE UNIVERSITY

Pheasant Curry

SERVES 6

We find it is best to cook this, leave it overnight and have it the next day.

Half cup decent quality vegetable oil
6-8 large garlic cloves, chopped
2-4 tablespoons cayenne powder
3 teaspoons ground cumin seed
1 teaspoon powdered ginger
Half cup tomato paste, mixed with
6 tablespoons water
Half teaspoon whole cardamom seeds, de-podded
2 tablespoons lemon juice
Half teaspoon salt
3 large onions – chopped finely
5 teaspoons garam masala
3 teaspoons ground coriander seed
2 teaspoons turmeric
6 pheasant breasts – diced

In a large, heavy skillet or a big cooking pot with a lid, heat the oil until it is fragrant. Add the onion and sauté over high heat, stirring frequently – until it starts to brown a little, about 4 minutes. Lower the heat and continue cooking, stirring often, until the onion turns golden brown, about 10 minutes more. Add the garlic, garam masala and cayenne. Lower the heat to medium-high, and sauté for another 2 minutes. Stir in the ground spices and sauté another 2 minutes, stirring. Add the meat, stir well, and brown it in the spices for about 5 minutes. Add the tomato paste mixture and cardamom seeds and stir well. Lower heat, cover pan tightly, and simmer for about 30 minutes, stirring occasionally and adding more water by teaspoon if sauce starts to stick to the pan.

Uncover the pan and stir in the lemon juice and salt. Simmer uncovered for about 10 minutes longer, stirring frequently, until the meat is tender and the sauce is very thick. You may then serve it with some rice and the usual accoutrements.

Kevin Parker
MILL OF FINTRAY, ABERDEENSHIRE

Roast Pheasant Stuffed with Orange

SERVES 3

1 pheasant
1 medium orange
3 slices bacon
55ml sherry
4 cloves
Olive oil spray
Freshly ground salt and pepper

Preheat oven to 200°C, gas mark 6.
Peel orange and divide into quarters. Sprinkle a little salt and pepper, plus cloves into the pheasant's breast cavity. Spray cavity with olive oil or put in a small pat of butter.

Stuff 3 of the orange quarters into the breast cavity and the fourth into the crop. Pour a little sherry into the cavity. Secure with wooden cocktail sticks.Sprinkle bird with salt and pepper and spray with olive oil. Cover with the pieces of bacon. Place on a trivet in a roasting tin. Add sherry and 75ml water to the roasting pan. Place in the oven. Roast for about 45 minutes or until pink – not overcooked. It will go on cooking for a few minutes after you take it out of the oven. For

pheasants in their skins: remove bacon after 30 minutes and sprinkle breast with flour and spray with olive oil and return to oven until the skin is golden brown and crisp.

Jean Lindesay-Bethune
ELIE, FIFE

Pheasant Phondue

If you phancy a really juicy pheasant that is moist and succulent, and so easy to cook, try this one for size...

Take a pheasant and skin it, cut off the breasts and thigh meat and chop them into skewerable chunks, make stock with the bones and use the stock to cook the meat chunks in! While you wait for the stock to cook make some dips for the phondue using mayonnaise as a base adding things like chutney, ketchup, mustard, etc.

It is simply the best way to eat those phlipping phlappers!

Alasdair Hilleary 'Loon'
REDCASTLE, ROSS-SHIRE

TIP...
Cooking lesson No 1:
Don't fry bacon
in the nude

Lazy Duck with Orange

SERVES 2

2 tablespoons butter
Marjoram
Parsley
Half an orange
1 duck
Thick cut marmalade
Juice of 2 oranges
Little stock or water
Freshly ground salt and pepper
Squeeze of lemon

Preheat oven to 180°C, gas mark 4.
Put the duck into a roasting dish. Place a large lump of butter, herbs and orange inside the duck. Spread the duck with butter and marmalade (rather like toast for breakfast!). Put the orange juice into the bottom of the dish and add a little water or stock. Cover loosely with foil and place in preheated oven for about half to three quarters of an hour. Baste frequently, adding more juice, water or stock if necessary, until the bird is how you like it.

If it is an older bird you may do this in a lidded casserole and cook it in a slower oven for longer, but keep basting. When the bird is ready, remove, keep and scrape up all the juices with any brown bits. Taste to see what it needs – probably salt, pepper and a squeeze of lemon.

Julia Ormsby
KILRIE, FIFE

Archduchess Anna's favourite Venison

SERVES 6/8

Saddle of venison
Good dry white wine
Juniper berries
Thyme
Bay leaves
Carrots
Onions
3 cloves garlic
Unsalted butter
Cognac
Game stock
Redcurrant jelly
Double cream

Take a saddle of venison. Bone the fillets (keeping the bones for stock) and cut the meat into thick steaks.

Leave them overnight in a marinade of the wine, juniper berries, thyme, bay leaves, carrots, onions and garlic. Make a stock with the venison bones. Fry the steaks in a frying pan with unsalted butter. Put them on a serving plate. Make a sauce with the pan juices, add Cognac, game stock, redcurrant jelly and a generous amount of double cream. Correct seasoning and pour over the venison steaks.

Serve with pasta shells and Chanterelles

Philip Astor
WITH A LITTLE HELP FROM MONICA VON HOUSEKEEPER
TILLYPRONIE, ABERDEENSHIRE

Pot-Roasted Pheasant with Cider, Apple & Chestnut Cream Sauce

SERVES 4

I serve this dish with parsnip mash and baby sprouts with toasted almonds.
A slice of caramelised Cox's apple makes a perfect garnish.

2 oven-ready pheasants
2 medium onions – chopped small
2 sticks of celery – chopped in small chunks
2 cooking apples – peeled, cored and sliced
12 whole shallots – peeled
240g tin of whole chestnuts (or prepare your own)
250ml dry cider
125ml double cream
Salt and freshly ground black pepper
2 sprigs each of fresh thyme, sage & parsley
2 shavings of orange peel
25g butter plus 2 tablespoonfuls of olive oil

Preheat oven to 200°C, gas mark 6.
Wash the pheasants, inside and out and pat dry. Season with salt and pepper. Make a small bundle of herbs for each pheasant and place it inside the cavity of the bird together with the orange peel. Heat the oil and butter in a thick-based frying pan and brown the birds all over. Set them aside. Soften the chopped onions and whole shallots in the same pan, add the celery and apple and stir together well. Season lightly. Pour the cider over the vegetables and heat through. Pour this mixture into a deep, ovenproof dish. Sit the pheasants on top of the bed of vegetables. Spread a knob of butter over each bird. Cover with greaseproof paper and foil to make a 'lid'. Put the dish in the oven and cook for 1 hour.

To serve

Remove the cooked pheasants from the dish and keep warm. Pour the remaining contents of the dish into a wide saucepan. Add the whole chestnuts. Bring this sauce mixture to the boil and then simmer slowly, with the lid off to allow the sauce to reduce and thicken slightly. Just before serving, add the cream. Check seasoning and stir in 2 teaspoonfuls of freshly chopped thyme. Heat through again. The finished sauce should be thick and chunky.

   Place a spoonful of sauce on each plate. Carve the breast meat and place it on top of the sauce. Check the leg meat for tenderness and serve it too.

Shirley Spear THE THREE CHIMNEYS RESTAURANT, ISLE OF SKYE

Roast Roe Deer Haunch

SERVES – DEPENDS ON SIZE OF DEER

1 haunch of roe-deer

For the marinade:
Sloes from making sloe gin (only if you
have some otherwise use a dash of gin)
1 onion
1 small orange
1 wine glass of orange juice
1 glass of red wine
Ground pepper
1 teaspoon of mixed herbs

Prepare the marinade by peeling and slicing
the onion and assembling all the ingredients
except the orange in a deep dish large
enough to hold the haunch. Place the
haunch in the dish and turn it a few times.
Slice the orange and place it on top of the
meat. Cover the dish with cling film and
allow it to marinate for at least a day, turning
it once or twice.

Preheat the oven to 200°C, gas mark 6.
Take up the haunch and brown it in a frying
pan on the stove top. This helps to seal the
juices in the meat. Place the joint in a large
oven proof dish and pour over the marinade,
add a large pinch of salt. Cover the dish. If
you don't have a lid use damp grease proof
paper and foil. (I believe, foil taints meat and
fish if used directly on it.) Turn the oven down
slightly and place the dish in the oven on the
middle shelf for 1 hour. Transfer the meat to
the carving dish. Strain the juices, taste and
thicken if you wish.

Anne Moore
NEWTONMORE, INVERNESS-SHIRE

Balmoral Venison, Hotch Potch Potatoes with Black Pudding, Shallots, Braised Red Cabbage with a Cassis Jus

SERVES 4

Venison
4 x 175g pieces of middle cut venison loin

Season the venison with salt and milled pepper, then seal in a hot pan with a little oil. Place on a tray and bake in a hot oven for 8-10 minutes, allow to rest.

Hotch potch potatoes
4 baking potatoes – thinly sliced
12 shallots – peeled and sliced thinly
4 slices of black pudding
75g grated Parmesan cheese
150 ml double cream
1 clove of garlic
Salt and pepper
Pinch of freshly ground nutmeg

Preheat oven to 150°C, gas mark 2.
Lay 2 layers of potato slices, season them and lay down the shallots which have been caramelised, arrange another 2 layers of potato and then the black pudding is crumbled all over, and then lastly arrange the rest of the potatoes in layers till finished, remembering to season them in between, boil the cream, nutmeg and crushed garlic and then pour it all over the top of the hotch potch. Place in preheated oven and bake for 35-40 minutes, when nearly cooked scatter the Parmesan cheese all over and glaze in the oven, press the cake with another tray and leave to cool. Cut into squares for reheating. Place in a hot oven for 15 minutes, or until piping hot throughout, prior to serving.

Braised Red Cabbage
450g sliced red cabbage
100g sliced red onion
125ml balsamic vinegar
60g brown sugar
Half a teaspoon mixed spice
Half a teaspoon ground ginger
1 crushed star anis
I glove of garlic
1 tablespoon redcurrant jelly

In a thick bottomed pan, sweat the cabbage and red onion on a little clarified butter. Now pour in the vinegar, and then the rest of the ingredients lastly. Put a tight lid on it and let it cook very slowly in the oven for 2-2 and a half hours, stirring everything around once or twice during the cooking. Red cabbage, once cooked, will keep warm without coming to any harm, and it will also re-heat very successfully.

The Milton Restaurant
CRATHES, KINCARDINESHIRE

Heart Attack

The symptoms of a heart attack vary slightly from one person to another. They range from a severe pain in the centre of the chest, to having mild chest discomfort that makes you feel generally unwell.

The pain often feels like a heaviness or tightness which may also spread to the arms, neck, jaw, back or stomach. Or it may affect only the neck, jaw, arms or stomach. You may also sweat, feel light-headed, feel sick, or be short of breath. Symptoms can be very mild and produce little discomfort. In some cases people mistake the pain of a heart attack for indigestion and may never report it to their doctor.

If you experience any of these symptoms, don't ignore them. Call 999 immediately.

Very common, typical symptoms...
- Central chest pain
- Pain in your arms, neck or jaw
- Feeling sick or sweaty
- Feeling short of breath

Less common, less typical symptoms...
- A dull pain, ache, or 'heavy' feeling in the chest
- A mild discomfort in the chest that makes you feel generally unwell
- The pain in the chest can spread to the back or stomach
- A chest pain that feels like a bad episode of indigestion
- Feeling a bit light-headed or dizzy as well as having chest pain

First aid:
- Make casualty comfortable and get emergency help
- Sit casualty in a supported position with knees bent (The 'W' position)
- If the casualty is fully conscious: Give them a 300mg Aspirin tablet to chew slowly provided there are no reasons not to give the aspirin and provided the patient is not under 16 years of age.
- If the casualty has any medication for angina, such as tablet or spray, then assist them to take it.
- Call 999, ask for an ambulance and say you suspect a heart attack

Monitor the casualty's condition and be prepared to give CPR
if they lose consciousness

Actions at the scene of road traffic collisions

Stop and help **Stay on scene until an ambulance arrives.**
Remain calm and ensure your own safety

Assess the 1-2-3 of any hazards to:
1. You - make sure you stay safe: keep off the road
2. The scene - park safely and turn off the engine. Stop approaching cars, signal to them from the pavement. Use a hazard triangle if necessary
3. The casualties – get help from bystanders. If it is safe to approach the injured person, do so, but don't move them

Check
A – Airway (Open)
B – Breathing (Listen for breath sounds)
C – Circulation (stop any serious bleeding)

Call 999

Do this as soon as you can or get someone else to do it while you deal with the casualties.

Let the Emergency services know:
- **Where you are (your location)**
- **What has happened (describe the accident)**
- **How many people are injured**

The Emergency service operator will ask more questions and give you some advice. Stay on the line until this has been done.

The Sandpiper 'just in case' kit

It is important to have a well-stocked first aid kit in the home to deal with minor accidents, injuries and illnesses.

What should I keep in my medicine cabinet?

ESSENTIAL ITEMS

Paracetamol and/or Ibuprofen
(tablets or children's syrup)
Aspirin (not for children or asthmatics)
Plasters – assorted sizes and shapes
Non-adherent wound dressings
(eg. Melonin)
Triangular bandage
Crepe rolled bandage
Safety pins
Sticky tape (eg Micropore)
Gauze swabs
Oral rehydration solution (eg Electrolade)
Mild laxative (eg Senokot)
Anti-diarrhoea tablets (eg Imodium)
Indigestion remedy (eg Rennies, Zantac)
Tweezers
Sharp scissors
Thermometer
Antihistamine tablets or syrup
(eg Piriton, Zirtek)
Small Torch
Surgical gloves
Clingfilm (for burns)
A note of any medication currently
being taken
Contact details of GP
Postcode, Grid reference or GPS if known

NON-ESSENTIAL ITEMS

Aspirin (not for children or asthmatics)
Arnica cream (for bruising)
Rescue Remedy (for shocks)
Optrex eye wash with eye bath
Hot and cold packs (eg frozen peas)
Muscle rub (eg Tiger Balm, Radian)
Decongestant (eg Sudafed)
Vicks Vaporub
Throat Spray (eg Vicks Chloroseptic)
Throat lozenges
Cream or spray to relieve insect bites or
stings (eg Wasp-eze, Pyrethrum spray)
Skin rash cream such as hydrocortisone
(not for children or on face)
Insect repellent
Antiseptic (eg Tea Tree oil)

TIP... V for W, B for B
Vinegar for Wasp stings
Bicarbonate of Soda for Bee stings

TIP...
Remember to read all instructions and contra-indications. Check the expiry dates on drugs and medicines regularly. Keep all medicines out of reach of children.

Many items used in medical care have expiry dates so be sure that you pay attention to these and keep your kit refreshed periodically.

If you, or the members of your family have any special medical conditions such as allergies, you should write that information down on a card and place it in your first aid kit so that, if you are incapacitated, it can be found by those trying to help. Any medicines for these conditions should be included in the kit together with emergency contact details.

TIP...
Bloody bread

For any cut or superficial injury that seems to be bleeding a little or a lot – clean under running water then take a big clump of bread and hold it tightly and then secure it (bandage, tape, cloth etc) over the wound. Leave it on for a couple of hours then remove under running water (helps take off the bread without hurting or pulling on the formed clot). The bread seems to have an effect which causes the bleeding to reduce miraculously and possibly leads to better healing. Really does work.

TIP...

If you're ill when your doctor's surgery is closed call NHS 24 on 08454 24 24 24 SCOTLAND or NHS DIRECT - 0845-46-47 ENGLAND
If you think the situation is life threatening you should call 999

This is a generic kit aimed at all motorists to keep them and the casualty safe until professional help arrives.

- Warning Triangle
- Fire Extinguisher
- Fluorescent waistcoat
- First aid book
- Note pad and pen
- Protective surgical gloves
- Torch
- Whistle
- Window punch/seatbelt cutter
- Scissors
- Survival blanket
- Gauze swabs x 4

- Dressing bandages x 4
- Transpore/Micropore tape
- Triangular bandage x 2
- Steristrip wound closure
- Resuscitation face shield or mask
- Waterproof plasters
- Antiseptic wipes
- Safety pins
- Clingfilm (for burns)
- Antihistamine (eg Piriton)
- Rescue Remedy (for shock)
- Common sense

Adult basic life support

Check for danger
Make sure the victim, any bystanders, and you are safe

Look for response
'Shake & shout'

Shout for Help!
If patient not responsive

Open airway
Turn the victim on their back; place your hand on their forehead and gently tilt their head back. With your finger tips under the victims chin, lift to open their airway

Check breathing
Look, listen and feel for no longer than 10 secs

Obtain help
If the victim is not breathing ask someone to call for an ambulance or, if you are on your own, do this yourself; you may need to leave the victim to do this

Chest compressions
If their are no signs of life commence 30 chest compressions at the correct rate (100 compressions/min) and at the correct depth (4-5 cm)

Rescue breaths
After 30 chest compressions open the airway again using head tilt and chin lift.
Pinch the soft part of the victims nose.
Allow their mouth to open and administer 2 effective breaths
(ie blow steadily into their mouth whilst watching for a chest rise;
then take your mouth away and allow the victims chest wall to fall;
take another breath in and blow into the victims mouth once more)

Continue with 30:2 ratio of
Chest compressions: rescue breaths

Continue until help arrives or victim starts normal breathing

pork

Pork *n.* **1**. the flesh of pigs used as food. (from Old French *porc*, from Latin *porcus* pig.) **2**. **porky** *Brit. slang,* a lie. Also called: **pork pie**, (from rhyming slang *pork pie* lie).

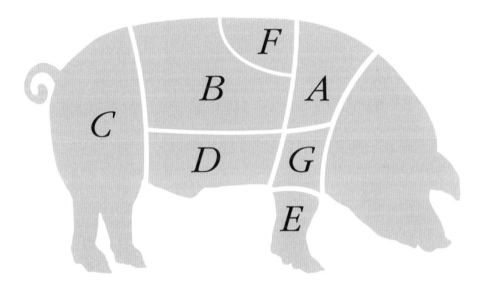

A Shoulder – roast

B Mid loin – roast, grill, fry

C Rump, leg – roast, braise, stew, cure, smoke

D Spring – spare-ribs, side bacon, belly – roast, grill, fry, cure, smoke

E Hock – roast, braise, stew, cure, smoke

F Rib loin – roast, grill, fry

G Fore shoulder – roast, fry, grill

Sausage, Pork and Bacon Casserole

SERVES 4/6

450g pork sausages
2 pork chops – sliced
4 rashers bacon – chopped
1 or 2 cloves garlic – crushed
2 onions – chopped
1 leek – sliced
Carrots & swedes – cut into fingers
Half a cabbage – shredded
4 medium potatoes – boiled – or baby new potatoes
2 tins tomatoes
Chopped parsley

Sauté the onions, garlic, bacon and chops, add the leek, carrot, swede and cabbage. Sauté for a further 5 minutes. Add the tomatoes and simmer gently for 30 minutes. Fry or grill the pork sausages then add them with the potatoes – cut into large pieces if using the larger potatoes. Stew and simmer gently for 10- 15mins.

Mag Leonard
INVERURIE, ABERDEENSHIRE

Chilli Pork Tortillas

SERVES 4

450g pork fillet – cut into thin strips
1 teaspoon ground coriander
1 red fresh chilli – deseeded and chopped
1 clove garlic – crushed
4 tablespoons lime juice
2 teaspoons sunflower oil
75g onions – thinly sliced
400g canned red kidney beans – rinsed
150g beef tomatoes – skinned, deseeded and diced
Salt and black pepper
8 flour tortillas
To serve
4 tablespoons low fat natural yoghurt
2 tablespoons chopped fresh mint
2 limes cut into wedges.

Place the pork into a bowl with coriander. Add the chilli, garlic and lime juice, toss well to coat meat evenly. Cover and leave to marinate for 30 minutes.
　　Heat the oil in a frying pan or wok and fry the onions over a medium high heat for 3-4 minutes until just beginning to brown, stirring frequently. Add the marinated pork and continue cooking for further 10 minutes or until meat is lightly browned. Add the kidney beans and tomatoes to the pan, season well and simmer for 3-4 minutes until tomatoes have softened.
　　Heat the grill to high then warm tortillas through for about 1 minute turning once. Divide the pork between the tortillas. Top each one with yoghurt and mint. Fold tortillas over and serve them with lime wedges.

Anne Watson
PERTH

Potato, Bacon and Onion Hotpot

SERVES 6/8

A hearty supper for hungry students.

900g potatoes – peeled and thickly sliced
225g streaky bacon – cut into 2.5cm pieces
450g onions – peeled and thinly sliced

For the sauce
50g butter
50g flour
850ml milk
1 dessertspoon of mustard – Dijon is best
A shake of Worcestershire sauce
50g mature cheddar
Freshly ground salt and pepper

Preheat oven to 150°C, gas mark 2.
Butter a deep pie dish using some extra butter. Layer the tatties, onions and bacon, ending with tatties on top.

Make a cheese sauce by melting the butter in a pan, adding flour and stirring over a medium meat for a minute or two. Take off the heat and add the milk. Return to the heat and stir constantly until the sauce bubbles and cooks. Add the cheese (off the heat or it will go stringy) and stir until it melts. Add a good dash of Worcestershire sauce (essential in a cheese sauce). Season.

Pour the sauce over the layers of tatties, bacon and onion and give the dish a shake to ensure the sauce runs down to the bottom. Sprinkle grated cheese on top.

Bake for 1 hour covered and 45 minutes uncovered until golden. Delicious with Sweet Chilli sauce and a huge mixed salad.

Joanna Aberdeen
HADDO, ABERDEENSHIRE

Barbecue Spare Ribs

SERVES 6

1.5kg spare ribs
4 tablespoons tomato ketchup
2 tablespoons French mustard
4 tablespoons honey
2 tablespoons Worcestershire sauce
2 tablespoons wine vinegar

Preheat oven to 200°C, gas mark 6.
Place the ribs in a large baking tray and cook in a hot oven for 20 minutes. Meanwhile mix all the other ingredients together and pour over the ribs. Return to the oven and lower the temperature. Cook for one and a half hours turning occasionally. Serve hot.

Lynsey Brunton
ARBROATH, ANGUS

Lord's Leftovers

SERVES 4

Delicious and unbelievably easy.

Four good sized slices ham – thick
One good-sized onion – roughly sliced
White wine
Cream
Flat leaf parsley

Fry the onion in a little oil until softened. Put the ham into the same pan then add wine, cream and some pepper. (No need for salt which comes with the ham.) Serve with rice and sprinkle with chopped parsley.

Alexander Aberdeen
HADDO, ABERDEENSHIRE

Edith's pork

SERVES 4

When on a walking holiday in Burgundy, I stayed with a lady called Edith and she served this dish after a very long hot day walking through the vineyards – a memorable occasion. It is a lovely supper dish which I make *en masse* for parties.

450g diced lean shoulder pork
1 medium onion
6 shallots
1-2 cloves garlic
About 8 stoned dried prunes
100g mushrooms
Butter
White wine
Chicken stock
Red currant jelly
Cream
Salt and pepper

Preheat oven to 180°C, gas mark 4. Brown the pork in a little butter over a medium heat and then remove. Chop the onions and shallots and sauté with garlic in some more butter. Add the pork, mix together and add enough white wine to come half way up the pork then cover with some chicken stock. Season with salt and freshly ground pepper. Place in casserole dish, cover and cook slowly for about one and a half hours.

Add the prunes and sliced mushrooms half way through the cooking process. I find it best to cook this dish to this stage, either the day before required or in the morning as the flavour develops.

Reheat for 20 minutes and add about 4 tablespoons of double cream before serving. To do this, take out some of the hot sauce, add the cream then stir back into the pork. This can be accompanied by pasta or rice and sprinkled with freshly chopped parsley.

Jim and Jean Royan
JIM IS CHAIRMAN OF NHS GRAMPIAN
PLUSCARDEN, MORAYSHIRE

Highland Pork

SERVES 3/4

1 pork fillet – sliced
50ml whisky
Plain flour
250ml cream
Parsley
Salt and pepper to taste

Marinate slices of pork fillet in whisky for 24 hours.

Take the pork out of the whisky and coat the slices in flour – keep excess whisky. Fry the pork slices in butter until they are just browning, add the left over whisky, fresh cream, chopped parsley and salt and pepper to taste. Serve with rice, a green vegetable and carrots.

Rob Collins
FARNHAM, SURREY

TIP...
Rest roast meat for at least 15 minutes before carving

Pan Fried Paprika Pork

SERVES 4

600g pork fillet
2 tablespoons olive oil
3 onions – thinly sliced
2 tablespoons paprika
300ml chicken stock
100ml crème fraiche
Freshly chopped parsley

Heat two tablespoons of oil in a pan. Add the onions and fry for 10-15 minutes, stirring occasionally – until softened and slightly coloured.

Cut the pork into bite-sized pieces, then add to the pan. Stir over a fairly high heat to seal and brown all over. Stir in the paprika, cook briefly, then add the stock and bring to boil. Cover and cook for 30 minutes, until the pork is tender. Stir in the crème fraiche and simmer for a further 2 minutes. Sprinkle parsley over pork before serving with rice and green salad.

Claire Maitland
CRATHES, KINCARDINESHIRE

Pork Chops with Cheese and Mustard

SERVES 4

4 pork chops
200g grated cheese
3 teaspoons wholegrain mustard
Double cream
Freshly ground salt and pepper

Heat a frying pan and brown the pork chops on all sides making sure that the fat is well cooked, this will take about four minutes. Turn on the grill to its highest heat. Mix the cheese with the mustard and enough cream to make a spreadable paste, season it with some salt and pepper. Spread the mixture over the chops and place under the grill for about 4 minutes until golden brown.

Puddledub Pork
AUCHTERTOOL, FIFE

Rocky Mountain Pork

SERVES 6

Half a cup fresh lemon juice
Half a cup soy sauce
6 tablespoons honey
2 small shallots – peeled and halved
2 large garlic cloves – peeled and halved
2 bay leaves – crumbled
Half a teaspoon salt
2 teaspoons freshly ground black pepper
1 teaspoon dry mustard
1 tablespoon fresh ginger root – minced
1 teaspoon fresh parsley – chopped
1.35kg pork tenderloin

Combine the lemon juice, soy sauce, honey, shallots, garlic, bay leaves, salt, pepper, mustard and parsley in a food processor. Purée and pour over the tenderloin. Turn to coat the meat.
Cover and marinate overnight in fridge.
Preheat the barbecue on high. Place the pork on the grills and reduce the heat. Cook for 20 minutes. Let it stand for 5 minutes and

slice into medallions. Heat the reserved marinade in a pan until boiling. Serve with the pork

Fiona Chamberlain
COMBER, CO. DOWN, NORTHERN IRELAND

Roast Pork Fillet

SERVES 3/4

1 large pork fillet
Large tablespoon of olive oil
Large tablespoon of sweet chilli sauce
Glass of white wine
Squeeze of lemon
Salt
Lots of black pepper

Pour all the ingredients over the pork fillet and roast in quite a hot oven for 30 - 40 minutes. Slice and serve with rice and salad or new potatoes and peas.
Tip You can put the marinade on the fillet in the morning and just pop in the oven 40 minutes before serving. The juices are delicious and you can thicken them and make gravy or add creme fraiche and pour over pork. Add thyme or rosemary if you have them.

Suzanne Drysdale
KILRIE, FIFE

Roast Rolled Leg of Pork with Sesame Potatoes and Apple Sauce with Wild Garlic

SERVES 8 DEPENDING ON SIZE OF PORK LEG

Rolled leg of pork with skin deeply scored
Potatoes – peeled
Tablespoon of sesame seeds
Oil for roasting
2 or 3 Bramley apples – peeled and sliced
Some diluted elderflower cordial or water
1 dessertspoon brown sugar
Wild garlic – if available

Preheat oven to 200°C, gas mark 6.
Leave the pork at room temperature for an hour to take the chill off. Rub the pork skin with salt and some olive oil. Cook for 20 minutes to half an hour until the skin is beginning to 'crackle' but not too brown. Turn the oven down to medium – 180°C, gas mark 5 and roast for a further hour. Allow 30 minutes per kilo for the meat. Leave to rest in a warm place for 15 minutes.
    Toss the potatoes in sunflower oil and put into a hot roasting tin and cook for an hour or until brown. 15 minutes before they are cooked sprinkle with sesame seeds and return to the oven – don't let them burn.
    Cook the apples in a saucepan with elderflower cordial or water and the brown sugar. Cook until just soft and beginning to break up. Take off the heat and mix in 10 leaves of washed wild garlic - shredded. Serve with a green vegetable, for example, cabbage or spinach.

Puddledub Pork
AUCHTERTOOL, FIFE

Slow Roast Shoulder of Pork

SERVES 8

The shoulder is ideal for long slow cooking. It is ideal as a lazy Sunday lunch dish since all the work is done the night before!

Shoulder of pork about 1.8 kg
12 garlic cloves – peeled and crushed
100g of fennel seeds – crushed
Freshly ground salt and pepper
4 or 5 dried red chillies
Juice of 6 lemons
4 tablespoons olive oil

Have a hot oven ready 230°C, gas mark 8. Make slashes across the shoulder skin. I use a Stanley knife since you can set the blade to a half inch depth and it won't go any deeper. The slashes should be about .5cm apart.

Lightly crush the chillies with the garlic and fennel, mix in salt and pepper. Rub this all over the skin of the meat and roast in the hot oven for about half an hour. This should be enough time to blister the skin and it should start to go brown.

Mix half the lemon juice with 2 spoons of the oil and pour all over the meat. Reduce the heat to 120°C, gas mark 2, or transfer to the simmering oven of an Aga and leave overnight or all day – certainly at least 8 hours. Turn the meat occasionally and baste with more lemon and oil.

The meat is ready when it falls off the bone or is soft under the skin, which should be crisp. The juices left in the pan provide the sauce, add the remaining lemon juice or oil.

Puddledub Pork
AUCHTERTOOL, FIFE

Francoise's quick bacon quiche

SERVES 4

110g plain flour
4 eggs
570ml milk
Smoked bacon, streaky or off cuts
– enough to cover bottom of dish.
50g grated cheese

Preheat oven to 200°C, gas mark 6.
Mix the milk, flour, eggs, cheese, salt and pepper in a liquidiser or blender.
Put the bacon in an ovenproof dish – about 20cm diameter and pour the mixture over the top. Cook in a preheated oven for about half an hour. Good hot or cold.

Jenny Bond
DUNECHT, ABERDEENSHIRE

Wiltshire Pork Casserole

SERVES 6/8

2 tablespoon sunflower oil
1.4kg shoulder of pork cut into 3.5cm cubes
50g plain flour
425ml chicken stock
4 tablespoons white wine vinegar
3 tablespoons clear honey
2 tablespoons soy sauce
225g large mushrooms – quartered
225g ready to eat stoned prunes
Freshly ground salt and pepper
Parsley to garnish

Preheat oven to 180°C, gas mark 4.
Heat the oil in a large flameproof casserole.

Add the pork in batches and cook over a medium heat for 5 minutes or until brown. Return all the meat to the casserole and add the flour. Cook for one minute. Add the stock, vinegar, honey, soy sauce, salt and pepper and bring to the boil. Cover and cook in the preheated oven an hour and 45 minutes. Stir in the mushrooms and prunes and cook for another half an hour or until pork is tender.

V. Reid
DOUNE, PERTHSHIRE

Sausage Hotpot

SERVES 4

A great store cupboard supper that makes sausages much more interesting and warms the body up!

1lb favourite sausages - left whole or cut into 3
1 onion – chopped
1 tin baked beans
1 tin kidney beans – drained and rinsed
1 tin chopped tomatoes
1 tablespoon oil

Preheat oven to 170°C, gas mark 3. Heat the oil in a casserole and brown the onions and sausages. Add the baked beans and kidney beans. Sieve the tin of tomatoes into the mixture. Cook slowly on the hob or in the oven for 30 -40 min. Great served with mashed potatoes.

Claire Smart
TORPHINS, ABERDEENSHIRE

Pork chops in a sticky sauce with baked potatoes

SERVES 2

One of the easiest suppers around and it turns out different everytime... take care not to burn it as it has sugar in the recipe.

2 potatoes, not too big
– Maris Piper are fab
2 large pork chops
2 cloves garlic – chopped
1 nub of ginger – chopped
2 shallots – chopped
I red chilli – seeded and chopped
2 tablespoons Worcestershire sauce
4 tablespoons soy sauce
2 tablespoons brown sugar
2 tablespoons tomato purée
1 tablespoon Encona sweet chilli sauce
– if you like it extra hot

Preheat oven to 200°C, gas mark 7. Rinse and spike the potatoes – oil and salt them if you like and shove them in the oven.
    While they are cooking, put the pork chops into a shallow, ovenproof dish. Combine all the other ingredients into a bowl. Start with the sugar as then you only have one spoon to wash up. Pour the dark mixture over the chops and put in the oven with the potatoes.
    Everything should be done at the same time – about 25 minutes later. Have some broccoli and sugar snap peas steamed and ready to eat.

Fiona Hill
GLASS, ABERDEENSHIRE

lamb

Lamb n. **1**. the young of a sheep. **2**. the meat of a young sheep. **3**. a person, esp. a child, who is innocent, meek and good, etc **4**. **like a lamb to the slaughter** without resistence, innocently.

Aromatic Lamb with Lentils

SERVES 6

1.35kg lamb, good stewing cut.	**For the marinade**
2 tablespoon olive oil	150ml orange juice
2 onions – chopped	2 tbsp olive oil
110g brown lentils (puy lentils)	Cloves garlic – crushed
175g ready to eat apricots	1 teaspoon ground ginger
570ml lamb or chicken stock	1 teaspoon ground coriander
Freshly ground salt and pepper	Half teaspoon cinnamon

First make the marinade
In a large bowl combine the orange juice, olive oil garlic, ginger, coriander and cinnamon. Cut the lamb into chunks. Submerge in the marinade, cover loosely and leave to marinate in the fridge overnight.

Preheat oven to 160C, gas mark 3.
Remove the lamb from the marinade, reserving the marinade. Heat the olive oil in a large flameproof casserole, and cook meat over a high heat for 5 minutes to brown all over. Lift out the lamb chunks with a slotted spoon. Lower the heat slightly. add the onions, and cook gently, stirring occasionally, for a few minutes until just soft but not coloured. Lift out of the casserole. Put lamb, onions, apricots and lentils into the casserole, pour in the stock and reserved marinade. Add salt and pepper to taste. Bring to the boil. Cover and cook in the preheated oven for approximately 1 to 2 hours or until meat is tender.

Serve with plain boiled patna rice or new potatoes boiled in their skins, and broccoli. Delicious autumn and winter dish, very easy and foolproof!

Jean Lindesay-Bethune
ELIE, FIFE

Mediterranean Roast Leg of Lamb

Press several garlic cloves and anchovy paste with your thumb into a leg of lamb. Smear harissa paste generously all over and BBQ. Brilliant.

Geordie Burnett-Stuart
CRICHIE, ABERDEENSHIRE

Slow cooked Lamb

SERVES 6/8 DEPENDING ON SIZE OF LAMB

Leg of Lamb or 1 or 2 shoulders or several lamb shanks.
Chopped carrots
Chopped celery
Chopped onions.
Butter
Olive oil
About a dozen peeled garlic cloves
Large bunch of rosemary
Half a bottle of red wine
500ml water
Couple of lamb or vegetable stock cubes
1 or 2 tins drained and rinsed cannellini or haricot beans

Brown the lamb in a roasting tin in the butter and olive oil. Add the chopped vegetables to the pan and fry them a bit along with the garlic, shove the rosemary underneath the meat, pour over the liquids and stock cubes, bring to a simmer on the hob. Cover with foil or a lid and place in preheated oven for about 4 hours, turn the roast around every half hour or so if you feel like it. Take the rosemary bunch out and add the beans for the last half hour. Don't panic if you have to add more liquid during cooking, it doesn't matter if you have too much as, liquidised, it makes a fine soup.

Julia Ormsby
KILRIE, FIFE

Northern Spanish Lamb

SERVES 6

4 red peppers
2 tablespoons olive oil
1 boned shoulder of lamb
4 cloves of garlic
1 large mild onion – chopped
3 tomatoes
Bouquet garni
2 bay leaves
150ml dry sherry
Chopped parsley
Freshly ground salt and pepper

Preheat oven at 160 C gas mark 3.
Blacken the peppers and peel off skin, remove stalk and seeds and cut into large slices. Trim the lamb of any extra fat. Heat the oil in a large casserole and brown the lamb on all sides. Remove it from the casserole, add the garlic and onion and stir over a gentle heat until they soften but do not brown. Add the tomatoes, bouquet garni, and bay leaves. Place the lamb on top of the vegetables, season with salt and pepper and pour over the sherry. Bring to a boil, cover tightly and put in preheated oven. Cook for about 2 hours, turn the lamb over and cook for another 15 minutes. De-grease the juices and scatter with parsley

Julia Ormsby
KILRIE, FIFE

Greek Lamb with Lemons and Feta

SERVES 4

Half tablespoon olive oil
500g lamb fillet cubed
12 shallots peeled
2 cloves garlic
400g ripe tomatoes – roughly chopped
Zest and juice of 1 lemon
400ml of lamb stock
Freshly ground salt and pepper
450g Charlotte new potatoes – cut into bite size pieces
2 tablespoons fresh parsley
80g feta cheese – crumbled
1 lemon cut into 4 wedges, to serve

Heat oil in a good quality, large, lidded, non-stick frying pan, add the lamb and shallots and cook over a high heat for 8 minutes, turning occasionally, until the meat has browned on all sides and shallots are tinged gold. Add the garlic, tomatoes, lemon juice & zest, stock and seasoning, stir well and bring to the boil. Reduce the heat, cover and cook for one and a half hours, then mix in the potatoes and cook for a further 30 minutes or until tender. Keep an eye on the stock level, as the potatoes soak it up, sometimes more stock is required.

Place in a large warmed serving bowl, scatter the parsley and feta over the top and serve with a green salad and rustic bread to mop up the juices.

Lisa Hector
ALYTH, PERTHSHIRE

Indian Lamb Chapattis

SERVES 4

500g minced lamb
4 chappattis
1 tablespoon each chopped cucumber, red onion and tomatoes
4 tablespoons low fat fromage frais
2 teaspoons paprika
A few fresh mint leaves

For the marinade
125g low fat natural yogurt
175g chopped onions
2 tablespoons fresh ginger – chopped
8 cloves garlic – chopped
2 green chillies – deseeded and chopped
6 sprigs fresh coriander
6-8 fresh mint leaves or
half teaspoon dried mint
Half teaspoon ground tumeric
1 and a half tablespoons ground cumin
1 and a half tablespoons ground coriander
1 teaspoon garam masala

Preheat oven to 200°C, gas mark 6. Put all marinade ingredients into food processor and blend to a smooth puree. Place minced lamb in bowl, add marinade and blend thoroughly. Cover and leave for 1 and a half to 2 hours or overnight in the fridge. Bring meat to room temp before cooking. Spread meat out evenly in a 25 x 20cm ovenproof dish and bake in preheated oven for 10 minutes. Remove from oven and break mince down with a fork into chunky pieces, then stir it thoroughly to absorb any cooking juices. Return to oven and continue cooking it for a further 15-20 minutes, stirring half way through till mince is browned and juice is absorbed. Spoon equal portions of lamb onto each chapatti, then top each with some chopped salad vegetables, and a little fromage frais. Serve garnished with a sprinkle of paprika and a few mint leaves.

Anne Watson
PERTH

Kofta Patties

SERVES 4

110g minced pork
450g minced lamb
1 teaspoon ground cumin
1 teaspoon chilli powder
1 teaspoon ground coriander
1 teaspoon ginger
2 cloves garlic – crushed
110g onion – finely chopped
1 teaspoon curry paste
1 egg beaten (optional)
Freshly ground salt and pepper

Combine all ingredients.
Form into small patties or kebabs.
Cook on BBQ, brush with a little oil.

White Cottage Restaurant
ABOYNE, ABERDEENSHIRE

TIP...
Laugh whenever you can, it is cheap medicine

Lamb and Rosemary Envelopes

SERVES 4

Looks great, to impress a hungry male or female – easy to prepare and can be frozen for an emergency meal.

4 boneless lamb leg steaks
1 tablespoon olive oil
Leaves from 4 sprigs of rosemary, plus 4 small sprigs.
375g pack ready rolled puff pastry
4 rounded tablespoons cranberry sauce
1 egg beaten

Preheat oven to 200°C, gas mark 6.
Season lamb all over and sprinkle with chopped rosemary.
    Heat the oil in a pan and fry the lamb for 2 minutes on each side till browned. Cool on a plate. Unroll the pastry and cut into 4 rectangles. Roll out each piece until large enough to enclose the lamb. Place the lamb steak on each piece of pastry then pop a tablespoon of cranberry sauce on each. Brush the pastry edges with a little beaten egg and fold over to enclose the lamb – pinching to seal the edge.
    You can freeze the parcels at this point, or prepare and chill up to 4 hours ahead. If not, place on a baking sheet and chill for 20 minutes to set the pastry – if time.
    Brush parcels with a little beaten egg, stick a rosemary sprig into the top of each one. Bake in preheated oven for 20-25 minutes until puffed and golden.

Claire Smart
TORPHINS, ABERDEENSHIRE

Bobotie

SERVES 6/8

900g best minced lamb
2 cloves garlic – chopped
2 bananas – sliced
2 apples – cored and cut into chunks
2 medium onions – chopped
2 bay leaves
50g shredded almonds
2 tablespoons curry powder
Chutney – I usually use mango chutney
or something but not Branston,
3 dessertspoons is usually enough
A little olive oil
4 slices bread without crusts
570ml milk
2 beaten eggs
Bay leaves/almonds to decorate.

Preheat oven to 180C, gas mark 4.
In a big saucepan fry the onion, meat and
garlic until browned in the oil. Chuck in the
other ingredients except the egg bread and
milk. Mix and cook for a few minutes.
Meanwhile soak the bread in the milk.
Squeeze the milk from the bread. Keep the
milk and then put the bread in with the
meat and mix in well. Once the meat looks
pretty well cooked through (about 15
minutes stirring occasionally) pour into a
deep pie dish. Take the milk and mix with
four eggs until custard like and pour this
over the whole lot. Decorate if desired and
then cook in preheated oven for about 50
minutes until top is golden.

Victoria Galey
MONTROSE, ANGUS

Headmaster's Lamb Chops

SERVES 2

Allow 2 chops per person. The lamb chops
should be sprinkled with salt, black pepper
and crushed garlic. Whack under grill at
highest heat for 2 minutes each side. Serve
with steamed asparagus and new potatoes
blobbed with butter and fresh parsley.

Michael Mavor
LORETTO SCHOOL, EDINBURGH

BBQ Lamb Chops

SERVES 4

For the marinade
1 large onion
1 cup red wine vinegar
Half a cup olive oil
1 teaspoon salt
Freshly ground black pepper
1 teaspoon of dried oregano

In a large bowl, combine all the marinade
ingredients. Put the meat into the marinade,
give it all a good shoogle to coat everything.
Leave in the fridge for at least 8 hours. Do
this in a plastic box if you are planning a wee
trip out, that way you can seal it and take the
whole thing with you.
Put the chops on the BBQ and cook for 5-10
minutes on each side, turning frequently and
basting with the marinade. Serve with naan
bread, and yoghurt salad.

Dr Kate Dawson
SOUTH UIST, BENBECULA

Moussaka

SERVES 4

700g minced Scottish lamb
2 large peeled onions – chopped
5 cloves garlic– pressed
2 carrots
2 red peppers – chopped
3 medium aubergines
2 tins organic chopped tomatoes
2 tins organic kidney beans
570ml semi-skimmed milk
110g margarine
110g organic plain flour
Grated mature Cheddar

Preheat oven to 180°C, gas mark 4.
Slice the aubergines thinly and lay on a baking tray pour over some organic sunflower oil and place in hot oven to cook. Remove when cooked (about 10 minutes) and cool.

In a large casserole dish fry the onions and garlic in some organic sunflower oil until soft, add the lamb and stir until brown. Add the peppers and carrots, stir in the kidney beans, add a little water or stock if necessary and cook in preheated oven for 30 minutes.

Melt margarine, add the flour and cook for a minute. Over a low heat, slowly add the milk and stir until it begins to thicken, now add the Cheddar cheese. Remove the mince and cover with chopped tomatoes. Place the sliced cooked aubergines on the tomatoes, cover with the cheese sauce and put in a hot oven until cooked to a golden colour. Before serving sprinkle with parsley. Serve with a green salad.

Diana Milligan
KINCARDINE O'NEIL, ABERDEENSHIRE

Spiced Stuffed Leg of Lamb

SERVES 8

Long slow cooking is best for this.

One whole boned leg of lamb
2 garlic cloves
1 teaspoon ground or fresh ginger
1 teaspoon chilli powder
Half teaspoon cumin
Half teaspoon paprika
Half teaspoon cinnamon
Salt
1 red onion
2 small pots plain yoghurt
Juice of one lemon
Handful of nuts, such as pistachio, pine nuts, sliced almonds
Handful of raisins

Preheat oven to 180°C, gas mark 4.
Chop up and mix together all the ingredients. Cover the lamb with the mixture – inside and out – and put in a preheated oven for about 3 hours.

You should end up with well cooked but deliciously gooey meat and lots of dark sweet brown sauce for the rice/couscous. Best served with a green salad and rice cooked with a few cardamom pods and a cinnamon stick added to the water or some plain couscous with a few chopped herbs such as mint, coriander, parsley. The juices are quite rich with the honey, yoghurt and onion and so it needs something quite plain to go with it.

Edward and Cath Baxter
GILSTON, FIFE

Nick is a typical laid-back teenager who does everything listening to his i-Pod. He got off the school bus and crossed the road without looking. The car passing the bus threw him 20-30 feet into a field.

When a colleague (also BASICS trained and Sandpiper bag equipped) and I arrived, his feet were almost where his knees should have been due to bilateral femoral fractures. As is always the case, the bag was invaluable immediately. Within a minute or so we had a cervical collar on, oxygen applied and quickly had venous access for expected fluid replacement and intravenous analgesia. Being able to separate the airway section meant that I could manage Nick's neck/airway (A & B) at the top end whilst Donna was sorting out 'C & D' lower down. With both of us being familiar with the layout of the bag, it made managing Nick's condition much less stressful.

I'm glad to report that Nick made a very good recovery and returned home about two weeks after his accident, walking with two sticks which he rapidly discarded!

GP, Haddo, Aberdeenshire

beef

Beef *n.* **1**. the flesh of various bovine animals, esp, the cow, when killed for eating. **2**. *informal.* human flesh, esp, when muscular. **3**. *slang.* to complain, esp. repeatedly: 'he was beefing about his tax'.

Carbonnade of Beef

SERVES 8

1kg rump steak – cubed
1 beef stock cube made up to 300ml with boiling water
2 onions– sliced
1 sachet bouquet garni
300ml beer
Pinch sugar
1 clove garlic – crushed
1 teaspoon vinegar
2 tablespoons oil
1 level tablespoon flour
1 French bread stick – thickly sliced and covered thickly with French mustard

Preheat oven to 170°C gas mark 3.
Heat the oil in a large pan, brown meat then put aside. Lower the heat and add onions and cook. Draw onions to one side of the pan, sprinkle in the flour then gradually add beer and stock, garlic, bouquet garni, vinegar, sugar and season. Stir all together until boiling. Put into a casserole and cover. Cook in a preheated oven for 1 hour 50 minutes. Remove from oven, stir and then push the slices of French bread on to the casserole, return to the oven uncovered for last 40 minutes.

Irene Steel
WICKERINN, KINCARDINESHIRE

Beef Goulash

SERVES 4

550g chuck steak
2 tablespoons dripping
1 tablespoon flour
570ml stock
1 garlic clove
2 large tomatoes
2 large onions
1 tablespoon paprika
1 dessert spoon tomato purée
Bouquet garni
1 red pepper
3 tablespoons sour cream or yoghurt

Preheat oven to 170°C, gas mark 3.
Cut meat into large cubes. Slice the onions, crush garlic into a cream with a good pinch of salt.
  Heat the dripping in a stew pan and brown the meat. Set the meat aside and lower the heat while you fry off the onions. Cook for a few minutes then add the paprika and, after a minute, the flour, tomato purée, garlic and stock. Stir until boiling. Then replace the meat and add the bouquet garni, a little salt and pepper. Cover and simmer gently on the stove or in a preheated oven for about 2 hours.
  In the meantime, shred and blanch the pepper, peel the tomatoes, removing the hard core and seeds, then slice them. When the meat is tender, add the pepper and tomatoes, simmer for 2 or 3 minutes and then turn into a casserole for serving. Spoon the cream over the top and serve.

Carol Mathewson
BURNTISLAND, FIFE

Beef Stroganoff

SERVES 2

250g beef fillet, trim and cut into strips
4cm x 5cm
1 small onion – finely chopped
1 clove garlic – finely chopped
30g butter
1 rounded teaspoon paprika
2 tablespoons oil
Salt and pepper
150ml crème fraiche

Melt butter in frying pan, add onion and cook over a low heat until soft and translucent. Stir in the garlic and paprika, cook for a minute. Remove mixture from the pan and set aside.
   Add the oil to the pan on a high heat. Add beef and cook until sealed and lightly browned. Stir in the onion mixture, season with salt and pepper and heat through. Swirl in the crème fraiche and serve immediately with rice.

Gordon Riley
PARAMEDIC, BANCHORY

Chilli con Carne

SERVES 2

This is best cooked the day before you need it. It tastes even better as the flavour comes out.

450g minced beef
2 medium onions – diced
1 tablespoon flour
Good pinch chilli powder
Tomato purée
1 tin chopped tomatoes
1 tin of kidney beans – rinsed
1 green and 1 red pepper

Brown the mince, add onions and cook for a couple of minutes. Stir in the flour, chilli powder, tomato purée and fry for a further 2 minutes. Then add the tomatoes, kidney beans and chopped peppers. Add salt/pepper and a beef stock cube to taste. Cook for a good hour. Serve with rice or nice crusty bread.

Debbie Sutherland
FALKIRK, FIFE

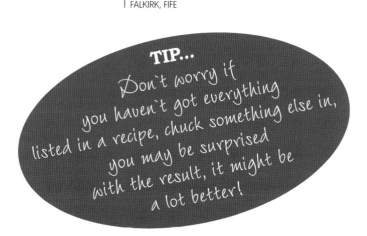

TIP...
Don't worry if you haven't got everything listed in a recipe, chuck something else in, you may be surprised with the result, it might be a lot better!

Homemade Beefburgers

SERVES 4

700g lean mince beef
1 onion – finely chopped
1 red chilli or red pepper or both – finely chopped
Freshly ground salt and pepper
Handful of mixed herbs
A good splash Worcestershire sauce
1 good squirt of tomato purée, Tommy K or sweet chilli sauce (or all of them)
Some breadcrumbs.
1 egg or two depending on large quantities

Mix all the ingredients together with your hands and shape into 4 burgers.

Emily Dickson
DOUNE, PERTHSHIRE

Boeuf Bourguignon

SERVES 4

Minimum effort, with maximum results. Yummy comfort food for those long winter nights.

2 tablespoons of olive oil
450g cubed beef
8 slices of thick smoked bacon – cut into strips
110g mushrooms
2 cloves of garlic – peeled and chopped
8 baby onions – peeled and left whole
6 sprigs of thyme
2 bay leaves
2 heaped tablespoons flour
1 bottle of red burgundy wine
Freshly ground salt and pepper

Preheat oven to 140°C, gas mark 1. Heat the oil and brown off the beef in an ovenproof casserole dish. Add the garlic, onions, bacon and fry off a little. Mix in the flour and stir in the wine. Then add mushrooms, thyme, bay leaves, seasoning and bring up to boil stirring all the time. Place in preheated oven for up to 2 and half hours. Serve it with boiled rice or mashed potato.

Annabelle Ollis
KINCARDINE O'NEIL, ABERDEENSHIRE

Corsindae Beef Stew

SERVES 6/8

2 tablespoons sunflower oil
1kg chuck steak – cut into 2.5cm cubes
3-4 rashers streaky bacon – cut into strips
1 large onion – chopped
45g plain flour
500g passata (you can buy this in
supermarkets - next to tinned tomatoes!)
450ml beef stock (cube dissolved in water)
150ml red wine
6 stalks celery – sliced
250g carrots – cut in thin strips
1 or 2 cloves garlic – crushed
Fresh marjoram (chopped) if available
(approx teaspoonful)
Fresh parsley – chopped

Preheat oven to 160°C, gas mark 3.
Heat oil in large ovenproof casserole. Brown
beef and bacon over moderate to high heat
for 2-3 minutes. (Should be browned all
over). Remove from casserole with slotted
spoon and drain on paper towel.
Next, cook onion for a few minutes, stirring
occasionally, until soft but not coloured.
Add flour and cook, stirring for a minute,
then add stock, red wine and passata. Heat
and simmer, stirring all the time until
thickened. Return beef and bacon to
casserole and add carrots, celery, garlic,
marjoram (if you have any), salt and pepper
and bring to the boil.
    Cover and cook in preheated oven for
about 2 hours until beef is tender. Garnish
with chopped parsley and eat!

Virginia Fyffe
CORSINDAE, ABERDEENSHIRE

Steak with Mustard Sauce

SERVES 4

Feeling rich?

4 sirloin steaks
2 tablespoons butter
2 tablespoons chopped shallots
Quarter cup cognac or brandy (a must!)
1- 2 cups heavy cream
1 tablespoon Dijon mustard
Salt and freshly ground pepper

Sprinkle both sides of the steak with salt and
pepper. Heat the oil in a large heavy skillet.
When the oil is very hot, add the steaks and
cook for 4-5 minutes on each side or to the
desired degree of doneness. Remove the
steaks to a serving platter, cover and keep
warm. Pour off the fat from the pan. Add the
butter and melt. When the foam has
subsided, add the shallots, cook about 1
minute. Add the cognac and flame it. Add
the cream and bring it to a boil. Cook over
high heat, stirring for 5 minutes. Remove
from the heat and stir in the Dijon mustard.
Taste and add some salt and pepper. Pour in
the juices that have accumulated from the
steaks. Fantastic!

Emily Dickson
DOUNE, PERTHSHIRE

Hot Steak Salad

SERVES 4

This can be a starter or main course depending on how large the portions are.

500g thin cut steak
750g salad potatoes
Salad leaves
Cherry tomatoes
Black olives
2 tablespoons dark soy sauce
2 tablespoons olive oil
3 tablespoons dry sherry
Balsamic vinegar
Sea salt
Salt and freshly ground pepper

Preheat oven to 170°C, gas mark 3, Cut the steak into strips about 1cm wide. Place in a bowl and mix with olive oil, soya sauce and the dry sherry. Leave to marinade for at least an hour.

Meanwhile, boil the potatoes for 10 minutes. Drain, then coat with olive oil and a little salt. Place in preheated oven for about 30 minutes. Pile the salad in the middle of each plate with the olives and tomatoes.

Drizzle with balsamic vinegar. Fry the steak in a hot wok or frying pan, stirring constantly. After a minute add the marinade that is left in the bowl and salt and pepper to taste. Fry briskly until the liquid is almost gone, but do not let it go dry. Place some potatoes round the edge of each plate.

Pile strips of steak on top of the salad. Drizzle with a little olive oil and balsamic vinegar and serve immediately.

Dr Neil Pryde
GP AND CMO OF KNOCKHILL RACING CIRCUIT

Jason's Steak with Broccoli

500g rib-eye steak
Broccoli
Fresh rosemary
Olive oil
Salt and freshly ground pepper

Preheat oven to 180°C, gas mark 4. About half an hour before you intend to cook the steak salt it liberally and add some pepper. Do this on one side of the steak only. Turn hob on as high as possible and with a grill pan sear the steak for three minutes on either side. Put the steak in the oven for 3 minutes, turn it over and heat for 3 minutes on the other side. Every time you turn it over add a little bit of olive oil. For rare this should probably be ok. Add some fresh crushed up rosemary and then leave to stand for five minutes.

While its standing, you can prepare a half floret of broccoli. And that's your 500g rib-eye steak with broccoli.

Jason White
ABERDEEN
SCOTLAND RUGBY CAPTAIN AND BRITISH LION

Mrs Robb's Stovies

SERVES 4

'The most well kenned stovies in north east Scotland'

Left over roast beef diced (or lamb)
12 medium sliced potatoes
2 large sliced onions

1 tablespoon cooking oil
or dripping from beef
A small amount of beef stock
Salt and freshly ground pepper

Preheat oven to 190°C, gas mark 5.
Gently cook the onions in small amount of
cooking oil until soft. Add sliced potato and
small amount of beef stock. Season with salt
and pepper and simmer until soft. Cook on
hob for about an hour or in a low oven.
Add cold beef and cook for further 10
minutes. Serve piping hot with oatcakes and
beetroot or chutney

Mrs Robb
CRATHES, KINCARDINESHIRE

Osso Bucco

SERVES 4-6

This best prepared a day in advance. Leave it
to cool and skim off any excess fat. Then
reheat and add the lemon, parsley, garlic bit
just before you serve it.

900g shin of beef (include some of the
bones if you can) I think you need about
225g of meat per person
4 tablespoons plain flour
2 cloves garlic, crushed
1 large onion chopped
150 ml beef stock (use a cube if you don't
have any)
150ml dry white wine
2-4 tablespoons tomato purée

Last minute
Grated rind of 1 lemon

2 cloves at least garlic finely chopped
2 handfuls of chopped fresh parsley

Preheat oven to 180°C, gas mark 4.
Put the flour with some salt and pepper into
a freezer bag. Cut the meat up into chunks
and toss about in the bag to coat it with
flour. Discard any excess flour. Brown the
meat in some olive oil, remove from the pan
and keep in a casserole. Soften onions and
garlic add to the beef. Pour in the wine and
stock and add tomato purée. Put the lid on
and cook in a preheated oven for about 1
and a half hours until the meat is very tender
and falls of the bones. This will taste pretty
dull until you do the next bit!
Chop up a couple of GOOD handfuls of fresh
parsley, a clove or two of garlic and the
grated rind off a lemon. When you grate the
rind off the lemon make sure you just use
the smallest grater size and JUST get the
yellow rind off.   Mix this all together and add
it to the stew and serve. It really makes the
dish.
    Serve with some really good mashed
potatoes and something green in the way of
vegetables.

Anne Pelham Burn
DESS, ABERDEENSHIRE

TIP...
The best way
to get the
last word
is to
apologise

Pesto Beef SERVES 6

Adapted from a recipe of Peter Gordon's from The Sugar Club. It is a family fav! Marinating is the secret to this – which can take up to a week. The pesto and garlic dressing can be made well in advance too.

1 piece of beef fillet, about 1.5 kg

For the marinade
500ml tamari (a type of soy sauce)
250ml cider vinegar
1 red chilli
3 cloves of garlic

For the garlic dressing
4 cloves of garlic
Quarter cup grainy Dijon mustard
50ml cider vinegar
Freshly ground salt and black pepper
110ml olive oil

For the pesto
3 cloves of garlic
4 handfuls of basil leaves
1 handful of flat leaf parsley
500ml olive oil
1 cup pine nuts, lightly toasted
1 cup Parmesan cheese

1 kg baby spinach, thoroughly washed

Get your butcher to trim the fillet. Put the fillet into a long dish. Whizz the marinade ingredients in a blender and pour over the fillet. Cover with cling film and leave it in the fridge for at least two days, turning every 12 hours. You can marinade it for up to a week.

To make the pesto Put all the ingredients except the Parmesan into a blender and whizz to a coarse paste – adding more olive oil if you need to loosen it. Turn it into a bowl and stir in the Parmesan. This will keep for a couple of weeks in a tightly sealed jar in the fridge.

To make the garlic dressing Put all the ingredients into a blender and whizz for a minute or so. This will keep in a jar in the fridge.

To cook the beef Preheat oven to 240°C, gas mark 9.
Drain the fillet and pat dry. Put it into a roasting tin and when the oven is up to temperature, cook the fillet according to your taste. While it is resting, put a scant amount of olive oil in the bottom of a large pan, heat and add the spinach, stirring until it has wilted. Drain it into a bowl and toss it with the garlic dressing. Slice the fillet and serve with the warm spinach and a spoonful of pesto. It is also delicious with creamy mashed potatoes.

Caroline Gladstone
GLENDYE, ABERDEENSHIRE

P's Beef Stew

SERVES 4/6

900g stewing steak
2 tablespoons flour
2 heaped teaspoons powdered
English mustard
Stock cube
Tomato purée
Ginger ale or beer and water
Onion
Carrot – optional
Celery – optional
Olive oil or other vegetable oil

Preheat oven to 180°C, gas mark 4.
Buy the cheapest, already cubed stewing
steak or get from a butcher. Put the flour,
powdered mustard, salt and pepper on a
plate and mix around. Dry the meat with
kitchen roll and toss in flour mixture.

Brown the meat in a saucepan with a
couple of tablespoons of oil. Put meat aside
on a plate. Cook onion and other chopped
vegetables – however much or little you
have or like – stir it around for five minutes.
Then pour in the liquid and stir. Add the
tomato purée and stock cube at the same
time. There should be enough liquid
to not quite cover the meat. You can add
potatoes, mushrooms, sweet potatoes – my
favourite, or any other vegetable at this time.

Cook in preheated oven for an hour.
If possible cook the day before and leave to
cool. Then just heat it up fully sometime in
the next 2 days.

Penny Dickson
DOUNE, PERTHSHIRE

Hell's Chilli Beef

SERVES 4/6

3 tablespoons olive oil
1 onion chopped
2 teaspoons good quality chilli powder
2 teaspoons ground cumin
1 teaspoon dried oregano
1 teaspoon dried chilli flakes (you can leave
these out if you think it will be too hot)
1kg rump steak cut into 2cm cubes
2 tins chopped tomatoes
500ml beef stock (use a Knorr
beef stock cube)
4 tablespoons tomato paste
1 tablespoon sugar
Salt and pepper

Garnishes
Red, yellow and orange peppers – chopped
Watercress – chopped
Chives – chopped
Cooked bacon – crumbled
Sour cream

Preheat oven to 160°C, gas mark 3.
Heat 2 tablespoons oil and fry off the onion
with the chilli powder, cumin, oregano and
chilli flakes for about 5 minutes – don't let it
burn! Add the rest of the oil and brown the
meat, in batches if necessary.
Stir in the tomatoes, stock, tomato paste and
sugar. Simmer, uncovered, or put into
preheated oven for about 1 and a half hours.
Keep an eye on it and put the lid on when
the mixture becomes thick. Season with salt
and pepper to taste.

Susan McGregor
EDZELL, ANGUS

"

Road traffic crash, Renault Scenic
versus HGV lorry, 3 people in
Scenic, driver (male) trapped by legs
and head injury, female front seat
passenger able to step out of vehicle,
no apparent signs of injury, 6 month
old baby boy, rear of car well
secured in baby seat, no apparent
injury but very distressed. We both
responded to this call and both used
our Sandpiper bags to administer
oxygen and apply cervical collars.
All 3 members of Scenic taken to
hospital, driver sustained base of
skull fracture and bruising, mother
and child uninjured. Lorry driver
treated at scene for shock.

GP, Aberdeen

puddings

Pudding (pudin) *n.*
1. a sweetened usually
cooked dessert made in
many forms and of various
ingredients such as flour,
milk and eggs with
fruit, etc.

After Eight Ice Creams

MAKES 10/12 RAMEKINS

350g After Eight Chocolates
50g caster sugar
6 egg yolks
275g double cream
Brandy to taste

Boil sugar in 225g water for 3 minutes. Put in blender with chocolate mints, blend until melted. Add beaten egg yolks and blend again. Cool. Add brandy and cream and blend again. Put into ramekins and freeze. Does not have to be taken out of freezer in advance of eating. (Make meringues with the 6 egg whites.)

Laura Wallace
STRATHDON, ABERDEENSHIRE

Apple Strudel

Shortcrust pastry
175g plain flour
Pinch salt
100g butter
1 and a half tablespoons caster sugar
1 egg yolk
3-4 tablespoons milk

Filling
700g cooking apples – peeled and chopped
1 rounded tablespoon currants
1 rounded tablespoon sultanas
2 tablespoons fresh breadcrumbs
1-2 tablespoons sugar – brown or white
1 teaspoon cinnamon

Preheat oven to 190°C, gas mark 5. Make pastry and roll out into a rectangle 23cm x 15cm and place onto baking tray. Mix the filling ingredients and pile in the centre of rectangle and fold over the pastry on either long side. The pastry will not meet in the middle and the apple mixture will be seen. Bake for 35-40 minutes. Dust with icing sugar.

Janey Heaney
MUCKHART, CLACKMANNANSHIRE

Balbridie Peaches in Champagne

Absurdly simple and effortlessly luxurious. The perfect way to round off a summer party or picnic.

Half a bottle of champagne or sparkling white wine
6-7 ripe peaches

Place the peaches in a bowl. Split a little of the skin of each with a sharp knife and pour boiling water over them. Leave them for a few minutes, then drain the water and peel off the skins. Slice or halve the peaches into a pretty glass bowl and pour over the champagne. Leave for a few hours to chill, then serve with whipped cream.
    Remember to finish off the bottle of champagne and why not go mad and open a few more!

Sheila Rhind
CRATHES, KINCARDINESHIRE

Bananas Flambé

PER PERSON

Bananas
Butter
Demerara sugar
Rum (or a similar spirit)

Melt a couple of grams of butter in a pan, when bubbling, throw in the bananas (chopped into 3 pieces halved). After about 1 minute, sprinkle 50g sugar over and stir. When the sugar has melted, pour in about 3 tablespoons of rum. Leave for a couple of seconds to heat up then light with a match. Serve with ice cream.

Simon Dickson
DOUNE, PERTHSHIRE

Butterscotch Sauce

100g soft brown sugar
100g butter
200ml double cream

Place butter and sugar in pan. Heat gently until sugar is dissolved add cream and boil for 3 minutes. This sauce will keep in the fridge for up to a month.

Patricia Haddow
ALYTH, PERTHSHIRE

Caramelised Nectarines or Peaches

6 peaches or nectarines
Soft butter
Demerara sugar
Ground cinnamon
Brandy
Crème fraiche or cream to serve

Preheat oven to 200°C, Gas Mark 6. Peel peaches or nectarines by dipping in boiling water to make skin easier to remove. Cut in half and remove stone (this is a bit of a fiddle but worth it and can be done in advance). Dry with kitchen paper and then rub rounded side of each fruit with soft butter. Put fruit into tight fitting dish and sprinkle with demerara sugar and cinnamon. Pour some brandy into dish around fruit and bake for 30 minutes until tender.

Virginia Fyffe
CORSINDAE, ABERDEENSHIRE

Cheat's Chocolate Sauce

2 Mars bars – roughly chopped
3-4 tablespoons milk

Melt the Mars Bars slowly over a gently heat, stirring frequently. When nearly melted and looking a bit globby, add the milk and continue to stir, Don't over cook as it will go chewy! Great poured over ice cream and worth scraping the pan!

Claire Smart
TORPHINS, ABERDEENSHIRE

Cara's Banoffee Pie

SERVES 6

A (450g) jar of Dulce de Leche - available from any good supermarket
20 digestive biscuits
100g unsalted butter – melted
3 bananas – sliced
300ml double cream – lightly whipped

Place the biscuits in a bag or a tea towel and crumble with a rolling pin. Put in a bowl, mix in the melted butter then spoon into a 25cm tart tin. Press the mixture down well to form an even layer before refrigerating for 1 hour.
Spread the biscuit base with the Dulce de Leche, a layer of sliced bananas and top with the whipped cream. Sprinkle with chocolate. Very yummy!

Cara Maitland
CRATHES, KINCARDINESHIRE

Chocolate Sauce

The quantities for this are vague – it all depends on how runny/chocolatey you want it!

Butter
Caster Sugar
Cocoa powder
Double Cream

Equal weights of butter and caster sugar melted over a low heat in a saucepan. Add cocoa powder (approx 1 heaped tablespoon per 25g of butter). Add double cream (roughly 2-3 tablespoons) to required colour/consistency.
Pour over vanilla ice cream, strawberries, chopped bananas or anything else. It can be made whilst the main course is being removed from the table. I have tried making it and keeping it warm but it can go a bit grainy – adding more cream or boiling water could sort that out though.

Deborah Rettie
RUMBLING BRIDGE, KINROSS

Chocolate Bomb

SERVES 6

450ml double cream
25g caster sugar
175g plain chocolate
25g butter
6 egg yolks
6 egg whites

Lightly whip the cream with sugar. Spread over the inside of a 3 pint basin using back of spoon. Place in the freezer until set.
Melt chocolate, add butter, stir until melted. Remove from heat. Add egg yolks and stir hard. Beat the egg whites until stiff and fold into chocolate mixture. Pour into the cream lined basin and freeze. Dip basin in cold water two hours before serving and loosen edges with knife. Turn on to plate and sprinkle with chocolate.

Eira Drysdale
NEWTONMORE, INVERNESS-SHIRE

Chocolate Mousse

SERVES 1/4!

225g best chocolate
6 eggs

Place chocolate in bowl over pan of boiling water - stir until liquid and smooth. Add yolks one-by-one, stirring with a wooden spoon. beat the egg whites then fold into the mixture. Leave to stand for 24 hrs. Serve covered with whipped cream.

Diana Macnab
LEUCHARS, FIFE

Crunchie Cream

Ideal for depressed times.

275ml double cream
3 Crunchie bars
1 egg white

Whip cream gently, beat egg white until stiff, crush the Crunchies, fold it all together and try to put it in the fridge and leave it for at least a couple of hours. Not easy!

Debbie Sutherland
FALKIRK

TIP...
What's
for you,
won't
go by you

Chocolate Tarte

SERVES 6/8

Small packet of dark chocolate digestives – crushed
110g butter – melted
225g cream cheese – Philadelphia is perfect
175g plain chocolate
110g caster sugar
150ml double cream
1 teaspoon vanilla essence
2 eggs separated

Preheat oven to 180°C, gas mark 4.
Melt the butter and add the crushed biscuits. Press into a loose-bottomed cake tin or flan dish. Bake in preheated oven for about 10 minutes. Leave to cool.
    Melt chocolate over a pan of water. Whizz cream cheese, sugar and vanilla essence, then add egg yolks one-by-one and finally the chocolate. Whip the cream and mix it in. Whisk egg whites and fold in gently. Pour it all into the base and leave to chill in the fridge for a couple of hours or all day. It freezes brilliantly.
    If you have put it into a loose bottomed cake tin you can run a hot knife round the edge and push the cake tin up from the bottom to turn it out. Don't worry about taking the solid bottom of the cake tin off, just serve it on a big plate surrounded by summer fruit or just more cream!

June McHardy
GLASSEL, BANCHORY

Easy Butterscotch and Chocolate Mousse

SERVES 6

2 x 100g Green & Black's butterscotch chocolate bars
275ml double cream
2 egg whites
Raspberries
A little whipped cream for decoration

Melt the chocolate in a bowl over a pan of boiling water. Allow to cool slightly. Partly whip double cream. Whisk egg whites. Mix cream into melted chocolate. Fold in whisked egg whites. Pour into 6 ramekin dishes and leave to set in fridge.
    Before serving, top with whipped cream and a good handful of raspberries.
NB. If catering for more people you can use Toblerone as a cheaper option.

Caroline Liddle
KINROSS

Easy Lemon Syllabub

SERVES 6

This pud goes beautifully with a small slice of Charlie's Malteser cake on the side! (See page 166)

Juice of 3 lemons and a little rind
900ml double cream
250g caster sugar

Boil the cream and sugar together in a pan and cook for 2-3 minutes. Add the lemon juice and stir well. Leave to cool slightly and pour into six glasses. Leave to set in the fridge. Grate a little lemon rind on top to decorate.

Suzanne Drysdale
KILRIE, FIFE

Elderflower Panna Cotta

SERVES 4

600ml double cream
10 or 12 heads elderflowers (no leaves as they are poisonous)
4 tablespoons caster sugar
2 small leaves gelatine (powder won't set properly)

Warm the cream with the elderflowers to boiling point. Take off the heat and leave to infuse for 3 hours. Put back on low heat and stir in sugar until crunchiness has disappeared.
    Meanwhile, soak the gelatine in water for a few minutes. Bring cream back to boiling point and sieve it. Squeeze water out of gelatine and whisk it into the cream until melted. Pour into small (big will not set) moulds or cups lined with cling film and leave in fridge to set for a few hours. Turn out and eat with cooked gooseberries or other summer fruit. Very little work for a very sophisticated taste.

Julia Wigan
KINBRACE, SUTHERLAND

Eton Mess

SERVES 4 – OR JUST ME!

450g strawberries
375ml double or whipping cream
50g icing or caster sugar
6 meringues

Rinse the strawberries, remove the tops and cut into halves. Break the meringues into small chunks and keep in a separate bowl.
Whip the cream in a bowl until reasonably stiff. Fold the sugar into the cream and add the strawberries. Just before serving, add the meringue to the mixture.

Anna Maitland
CRATHES, KINCARDINESHIRE

Fruit Brulée

SERVES 4

Greek yoghurt
Double cream
Raspberries or strawberries
Demerara sugar

Mix equal quantities of greek yoghurt and double cream and whisk until thick. Use this to cover fresh fruit in a flan dish (raspberries, strawberries etc) and liberally sprinkle with sugar. Put under the grill until the sugar has melted and formed a covering. Stick in the fridge to cool and serve from there. Dead easy, even for a bloke!

David Sole OBE
STRATHDON, ABERDEENSHIRE
FORMER SCOTLAND RUGBY CAPTAIN AND BRITISH LION

Clare's Fruit Brulées

A healthy and easy creme brulee.

Greek yoghurt
Créme fraiche
Raspberries, strawberries, Rhubarb
Muscovado sugar

Put a selection of fresh fruits into a ramekin three quarters from the top. Good ones are strawberries, raspberries, rhubarb etc. Stir together créme fraiche and greek yoghurt, then put a good dollop onto the fruit. Crumble some dark muscovado sugar over the top and either use a blow torch to caramelise the sugar or put high up into a hot oven to melt.

Clare Pelly
EDINBURGH UNIVERSITY

Granny Shepherd's Frozen Lemon Pie

SERVES 6/8

A recipe after my own heart being quick, easy and delicious!

Half a cup of finely crushed wholemeal biscuits for base and top
3 eggs – separated
110g caster sugar
225ml whipping cream
Grated rind and juice of a lemon

Sprinkle most of the biscuit crumbs into a well greased 23cm pie plate. Beat the egg whites until frothy. Gradually add the sugar and beat until stiff and glossy. Beat egg yolks

Granny Shepherd's Frozen Lemon Pie continued...

until thick and fold in egg white mixture. Whip the cream until stiff. Mix in the lemon rind and juice and fold into egg mixture.

Pour into the crumb-lined pie plate. Sprinkle rest of crumbs on top. Freeze. Remove from freezer 5-10 minutes before eating.

Lorraine Shepherd
Newburgh, Aberdeenshire

Grape Nut Ice cream

SERVES 4

An unusual ice-cream, discovered by accident – a variation of Victorian Brown Bread Ice cream.

Big tub of good quality vanilla ice-cream
Grand Marnier liqueur
Grape nuts

Melt ice cream to very soft but not liquid. Stir in, say, four tablespoons of Grand Marnier (alter according to taste) and a good pour of Grape Nuts. Mix in thoroughly and return to the freezer. Remove just before serving as liqueur will prevent it solidifying too much. The Grape nuts in the ice cream will remain crunchy for four or so days. Lovely with orange fruit salad, or raspberry coulis or fruit tarts.

Robert & Helen Harrison
FETTES COLLEGE, EDINBURGH

Hot Chocolate Fondant

SERVES 2

50g unsalted butter – plus extra to grease
2 teaspoons cocoa powder – to dust
50g good quality bitter chocolate (minimum 70% cocoa solids) broken into pieces
1 free range egg
1 free range egg yolk
60g caster sugar
50g plain flour

Preheat oven to 160°C, Gas Mark 3. Butter two large ramekins, about 7.5cm in diameter, then dust liberally with cocoa powder. Slowly melt the chocolate and butter in a small bowl set over a pan of hot water. Take off the heat and stir until smooth.

Leave to cool for about 10 minutes. Using an electric whisk, beat the whole egg, egg yolk and sugar together until pale and thick, then incorporate the chocolate mixture. Sift the flour over the mixture and gently fold in, using a large metal spoon. Divide between the ramekins and bake for 12 minutes. Turn the chocolate fondants out on to warmed plates and serve immediately.

Gordon Ramsay
THE F WORD

TIP...
Never tie your
shoelaces in a
revolving door

Jackie's Cookie Ring

SERVES 4

2 packets of chocolate chip cookies
1 cup of sherry (I usually use a dry one)
275ml double cream
A little chocolate for decoration

Whip cream until stiff, but not too dry. Put a little whipped cream in a circle on serving plate. (This is to hold the biscuits in place) Dip a cookie in the cup of sherry, then cover one side of the cookie in whipped cream, stand cookie on its edge in the cream on the serving plate.

Do the same with the next cookie sandwiching the cookies together with cream. Repeat with all the cookies until a ring is formed. Drizzle any remaining sherry over the biscuit ring. Completely cover the ring with cream, sealing the biscuits in. Melt a small amount of chocolate and drizzle over the ring or just grate chocolate and sprinkle over. Refrigerate until required.

This pudding is best made the day before you need to eat it.

Jackie Giles
LATHALLAN SCHOOL, JOHNSHAVEN, ANGUS

Jessica's Chocolate Fruits

MAKES ENOUGH FOR THREE GREEDY PEOPLE!!

1 bar of milk chocolate – broken into bits
1 apple
1 banana
12 strawberries
Also, you can add any other fruits you like

Melt the chocolate in a bowl over a pan of boiling water. Stir until smooth. Cut up the fruits and dip each piece into the chocolate. Place chocolate fruits in the fridge and wait for the chocolate to kind of stick.

Once the chocolate has hardened put the fruit around a plate. Eat and enjoy.

Jessica Foster (Age 12)
LONDON

Lemon and White Chocolate Surprise!

SERVES 4

50g butter
125g caster sugar
2 eggs – separated
25g self-raising flour
25g ground almonds
25g small white chocolate chunks
Zest and juice of 2 lemons
50ml milk

Preheat oven to 180°C, gas mark 4.
Cream the butter and sugar until smooth. Beat in egg yolks. Stir in the flour, ground almonds, chocolate, lemon rind, juice of 1 lemon and 50ml milk. Whisk egg whites separately, then fold into lemon mixture. Pour into individual ramekins.

Place in high sided ovenproof dish which is full of water. Bake for 25 minutes, until golden. The top will be a lemon and white chocolate sponge and underneath a lemon sauce. Serve with double cream.

Alex Bevens
ELY OR DURHAM UNIVERSITY

Lemon Curd Ice Cream

SERVES 4

500g tub créme fraiche
One and a half jars luxury lemon curd

Mix together lemon curd and crème fraiche.
Put into a lined 1kg loaf tin. Wrap in cling film
and freeze for 5 hours. Serve with
raspberries/strawberries or a fruit coulis.
Easy and delicious.

Debbie Spens
FETTES COLLEGE, EDINBURGH

Easy Apple Tart

SERVES 4/6

500g cooking apples
100g caster sugar
750g dessert apples (Cox's or Braeburns)
500g puff pastry (ready made)
175g apricot jam

Preheat oven to 200°C, gas mark 6.
Peel, core and slice the cooking apples, put
them in a pan with 75g caster sugar. Cook
over a low heat until tender. Tip apples into a
sieve over a bowl to reserve any excess
juices and mash apples with a fork. Leave to
cool. Roll out the pastry on a lightly floured
surface. Using a plate as template cut a
30cm circle. Move on to a flat greased
baking sheet. Leaving a 2.5cm border
around the edge, prick pastry randomly with
fork. Spread the apple purée on the top
leaving the 2.5cm border clear. Chill for at
least 20 minutes. Peel and core the rest of

the apples. Slice them very finely in half
moon shapes. Arrange the slices,
overlapping, in circles on top of the purée
and sprinkle with remaining sugar. Bake for
30 minutes or until the pastry is crispy and
edges of the apple are slightly browned. Put
the apricot jam into a small pan with left-
over apple juices – warm gently. Press
through a sieve and brush over apples.
    Serve warm or cold with cream or créme
fraiche. Best served on the day it is made.

Araminta Campbell
MARYCULTER, ABERDEEN

Magic Pie

SERVES 4/6

4 eggs
Half a teaspoon salt
1 teaspoon vanilla essence
225g white sugar
200g dessicated coconut
60g flour
500ml milk
55g margarine
Half a teaspoon baking powder

Preheat oven to 180°C, gas mark 4.
Place all ingredients in a blender and whizz
until fully mixed. Pour into a buttered 25cm
pie dish. Bake uncovered for 50-60 minutes.
When it's ready the pie emerges with a crust
at the bottom, a custard centre and a
coconut topping... as if by magic.

Dr Mark Bloch
ROYAL ABERDEEN CHILDREN'S HOSPITAL

Nectarines and Raspberry Coulis

SERVES 2/3

3 ripe nectarines – halved and de-stoned
1 punnet of raspberries
Kirsch

Briefly blanch nectarine halves using a fork in boiling water until skin can be removed – set aside. Purée the raspberries and sieve to remove the pips. Add small or large slug of kirsch to taste and pour over nectarines. Another winner!

Alistair Dickson
DOUNE, PERTHSHIRE

Oofum Floofum

SERVES 4/6

1 x packet flavoured jelly
1 x tin of evaporated milk, cooled in fridge
100s and 1000s

Whip up milk until thick in a mixer. Melt jelly and let it cool. Add jelly to milk and mix with spoon. Put bowl in fridge to cool.
Sprinkle with 100s and 1000s then kick it into touch.

Gavin Hastings OBE
PATRON OF THE SANDPIPER TRUST
FORMER CAPTAIN OF THE
BRITISH LIONS AND SCOTLAND

Orange Syllabub

SERVES 6

Juice of 2 large oranges and grated rind of 1
75g caster sugar
Juice of half lemon
275ml double cream

Combine the zest and juice of the oranges and add the lemon juice and sugar. Stir until sugar has dissolved. Whip cream until it begins to thicken. Pour into the juices and carry on whipping until thick. Pour into individual glasses or dishes and chill.

Lorna McGuire
ST CYRUS, ANGUS

Peaches or Nectarines in Honey and Lemon

SERVES 4

6 firm but ripe peaches or nectarines
2 tablespoons of runny honey
2 tablespoons of lemon juice

Remove skin from peaches (1 minute in boiling water) and cut into segments. Mix the honey with the lemon juice and marinate the peach segments.
Can be prepared 2 hours in advance.

.
Belinda Haig
SCANIPORT, INVERNESS-SHIRE

Pears in Red Wine

SERVES 4

150ml red wine
275ml water
150ml sugar
Strip of lemon rind
Cinnamon stick
6 pears – peeled and left whole with stalks

Stir wine, water, lemon and cinnamon stick over a gentle heat until the sugar has dissolved. Bring to the boil and boil briskly without stirring for 3 minutes. Add pears and poach (over a very gentle heat) for 20-30 minutes. Serve with cream.

Janet Duff
DOUNE, PERTHSHIRE

Pimm's Galore

DESSERT USING TWO TALL GLASSES

Pimm's
Sugar
Carte d'Or strawberries & cream ice cream
Crème fraiche
Mint Leaves

Place 4 tablespoons of Pimm's and some sugar in a jug. Place some Carte d'Or strawberries and cream ice cream into the glasses, followed by a layer of strawberries, then some crème fraiche. Continue the layers up to the top of the glasses. Pour Pimm's over top and add mint leaves

Laura Salisbury Jones
NEWCASTLE UNIVERSITY

Easy Cheesecake

SERVES 4/6

100g digestive biscuits
50g butter
25g demerara sugar
225g cream cheese
Small tin condensed milk
4 tablespoons lemon juice
150ml double cream

Crush digestive biscuits, melt the butter in a pan, add sugar then blend in biscuits. Mix well and line 18cm flan dish. Place cream cheese in a bowl and cream until soft. Beat in the cream and condensed milk. Slowly add the lemon juice and pour over biscuit base. Leave in fridge to harden.

Sue Bruce
FETTES COLLEGE, EDINBURGH

Relugas Pudding

Fresh fruit – fresh, stewed or tinned
Double cream
Low fat yoghurt
Soft dark brown sugar

Put a layer of fruit in the bottom of a serving dish or in individual ramekins. Mix equal quantities of double cream and low fat natural yoghurt and spread the mixture over the top – about 2cm deep. Crumble soft dark brown sugar on the top about an hour before you want to eat it . People who don't eat puddings can never resist this.

Panny Laing
LOGIE, MORAYSHIRE

Rum Log

SERVES 6

300ml double cream
1 packet of ginger biscuits
150ml rum

Whisk cream until thick (with some caster sugar to taste). Arrange biscuits in any fashion on a pretty dish (I lay them out overlapping in a log shape) and pour over the rum. Cover with the double cream and put in the fridge to set. Very boozy!

Debs Findlay
CARNELL, AYRSHIRE

Sticky Toffee Pudding

SERVES 8

225g caster sugar
225g self-raising flour
225g butter
3 eggs
1 teaspoon vanilla essence
225g butterscotch sauce (see below)

Sauce
1 block butter
1 capful scotch whisky
3 heaped tablespoons treacle
4 heaped tablespoons golden syrup
75ml double cream

Preheat oven to 190°C, Gas Mark 5. Prepare the sauce first, melting the butter over a gentle heat and adding the whisky, treacle and golden syrup. Mix until combined, remove from the heat and stir in the cream.

For the pudding itself, combine the sugar and butter in a bowl and add the eggs. Fold the flour in a little at a time. Add the vanilla essence and just under half of the butterscotch sauce. Mix well and pour the mixture into a suitably sized cake tin – preferably a loaf shaped tin. Cook for approximately 20 minutes. Turn out onto a baking rack to cool.

Cut a slice of the sponge and pour over a generous helping of the warmed butterscotch sauce. Serve with vanilla ice cream.

Kenny Logan
STIRLING
FORMER SCOTLAND RUGBY INTERNATIONAL

Strawberries Andorra

Slightly under-ripe
strawberries – cut in half
Pepper
Orange liqueur
Fresh orange juice

Melt the butter in a large flat pan. Add the strawberries seasoned with pepper and a good measure of liqueur. Set alight and flambé. Cook the strawberries until soft (but not collapsing) and remove to a warm plate. Add orange juice to the pan and reduce liquid mixture. Delicious with ice cream.

Dr Noelle Murphy
ACCIDENT & EMERGENCY CONSULTANT, RAIGMORE
HOSPITAL, INVERNESS

The Three Chimneys' Hot Marmalade Pudding

150g fine brown breadcrumbs
120g soft brown sugar
25g self-raising wholemeal flour (white self-raising would do)
120g fresh butter, plus extra for greasing the bowl
8 tablespoonfuls well-flavoured, coarse-cut marmalade (homemade is always the best)
3 large eggs
1 rounded teaspoonful bicarbonate of soda

Butter a 3-pint pudding basin well. Place the breadcrumbs, flour and sugar in a large mixing bowl. Melt the butter together with the marmalade in a saucepan over a gentle heat. Pour the melted ingredients over the dry ingredients and mix together thoroughly. Whisk the eggs until frothy and beat gently into the mixture until blended together well. Last of all, dissolve the bicarbonate of soda in 1 tablespoonful of cold water. Stir this into the pudding mixture, which will increase in volume as it absorbs the bicarbonate of soda. Spoon the mixture into the prepared basin. Cover it with close-fitting lid, or alternatively, make a lid with circles of buttered greaseproof paper and foil, pleated together across the centre and tied securely around the rim of the basin. Place the pudding basin in a saucepan of boiling water. The water should reach halfway up the side of the basin. Cover the pan with a close-fitting lid and simmer the pudding for 2 hours. The water will need topping-up throughout the cooking period. Turn out on to a serving dish, slice and serve hot, with fresh cream, ice cream, or as we do at The Three Chimneys – with Drambuie Custard...

Drambuie Custard

This is a proper egg custard with Drambuie liqueur. It's served warm, poured around the pudding. Alternative flavours could be added, such as vanilla, ginger or crushed cardamon – or try a tablespoonful of fresh ground coffee – delicious with chocolate desserts.

275ml fresh milk
275ml fresh double cream
6 egg yolks
100g caster sugar
2 tablespoonfuls Drambuie liqueur

Whisk the egg yolks together with the sugar until pale and creamy. Gently warm the milk and cream until it is just beginning to bubble. Pour the milk and cream onto the egg and sugar mixture and whisk. Return the mixture to the saucepan. Bring to the boil very slowly, stirring all the time. As soon as it begins to thicken remove from the heat and pour into a bowl or jug for serving. Stir in the Drambuie, or flavouring of your choice. Serve immediately.

Shirley Spear THE THREE CHIMNEYS RESTAURANT, ISLE OF SKYE

Vodka Jelly

1 packet of jelly – any flavour
Vodka

The idea of vodka jelly is a simple one: get drunk as quickly as you can. Make up a packet of jelly, using between a quarter and half of the amount of water suggested. Top up with as much vodka as you like (or can handle) and leave in the fridge to set.

Emily Dickson
DOUNE, PERTHSHIRE

Warm Peaches with Honey and Basil

SERVES 2

25g unsalted butter
2 ripe peaches or nectarines – stoned, skinned and thickly sliced
2 tablespoons clear honey
Juice of 1 orange
8-10 basil leaves – shredded
Vanilla ice cream or single cream to serve

Melt the butter in a non-stick frying pan, add the peaches and cook on both sides until slightly softened, approx 3 minutes. Add the honey and stir to make a sauce. Add the orange juice and bubble briefly. Stir in basil.
    Serve warm with cream or ice cream. This dish can be made up to 24 hours in advance and kept in the fridge. When ready to eat, flash through the microwave for 2 minutes on high.

Dr And Mrs Bill Steele
GRANTOWN-ON-SPEY

Yummy Crunchie Ice Cream

575ml whipped double cream
4 x Crunchies – smashed in their wrappers
1 x can of condensed milk

Mix the condensed milk into the cream. Gently stir in the Crunchies *et voilá* – a delicious pudding. Freeze and serve with some summer fruits.

Judy Shaw-Stewart
DOUNE, PERTHSHIRE

Lemon Soufflé Custard

This pudding separates into a gorgeous lemony custard with a light sponge topping.

4 eggs – separated
2 large lemons – juice and zest
225g caster sugar
25g butter
50g flour
475ml milk

Preheat oven 180°C, gas mark 4.
Blend the egg yolks, lemon rind and juice, sugar, butter and flour in a blender. Add the milk through a funnel. Beat the egg whites until fluffy and fold into the lemony custard. Pour into a greased ovenproof dish – make sure it's big enough before you start pouring!
    Place dish in a roasting tin surrounded with boiling water and bake like this for 35-45 minutes. .

Fiona Hill
GLASS, ABERDEENSHIRE

Don't allow children to lick out the bowl, they should flush it like everyone else...

cakes & biscuits

YUM YUM YUM YUM YUM

Cake n. **1**. a baked food, usually in loaf or layer form, typically made from a mixture of flour, sugar and eggs. **2**. **have one's cake and eat it** to enjoy both of two desirable but incompatible alternatives. **3**. **sell like hot cakes** to be sold very quickly or in large quantities eg The Sandpiper Cookbook

Biscuit *n*. **1**. *Brit*. a small flat dry sweet or plain cake of many varieties, baked from dough. **2**. **take the biscuit** *Slang*. to be regarded (by the speaker) as the most surprising thing that could have occurred.

Banana Cake

A wonderful way to use up old bananas and reasonably healthy!

4 medium bananas, mashed
250g self-raising flour
2 level teaspoons baking powder
100g butter (I use Flora)
220g caster sugar
2 eggs

Preheat oven to 180°C, gas mark 4.
Mash the bananas, then add all the rest of the ingredients. Use an electric whisk to briefly mix everything together. Line 2 x 450g loaf tins (I use Lakeland ready shaped liners) and divide the mixture. Stand tins on a grill rack in a roasting tin and bake in oven for 45 minutes.

Susie Pelly
FORDCOMBE, KENT

Banana, Walnut & White Chocolate Loaf

900g loaf tin
175g plain flour
125g unsalted butter
Half teaspoon bicarbonate of soda
Half teaspoon salt – optional
1 teaspoon baking powder
150g caster sugar
2 large eggs
4 small/3 large ripe bananas
100g white chocolate – broken up
60g walnuts
1 tsp vanilla essence

Preheat oven to 180°C, gas mark 4.
Rub tin with butter and dust with flour. Mix the flour, salt, baking powder and bicarbonate of soda in a bowl. Melt the butter in a pan and whisk in the sugar. Beat in the eggs one at a time, then whisk in the bananas. Add the chocolate, walnuts and vanilla then add dry mixture to wet in 3 stages. Pour into a loaf tin and bake for an hour – it's ready when it feels springy to the touch.

Kirstie Duke
ALFORD, ABERDEENSHIRE

Bara Brith (Tea cake)

356g sultanas or raisins
Half teaspoon bicarbonate of soda
58g butter
252 g soft brown sugar
300ml hot water
2 beaten eggs
366g self-raising flour

Preheat oven to 190°C, gas mark 5.
Put sultanas, butter and water in a pan, and bring to the boil. Simmer for 4 minutes. Allow to cool slightly. Mix together the flour, bicarbonate of soda and sugar. Mix warm fruit mixture into flour and add eggs. Grease 2 x 450g loaf tins and put in mixture. Bake in moderate hot oven for 1 hour. When it's cool slice and, if you like, butter – but it is very nice plain. Keeps exceedingly well wrapped in foil and in a tin.

Audrey Moore
BADACHRO, WESTER ROSS

The Best Uncooked Chocolate Fudge Cake

225g good dark chocolate – broken up
225g unsalted butter – cut into pieces
3 tablespoons brandy or black coffee
50g caster sugar
Vanilla essence
225g digestive biscuits – crushed
75g sultanas or stem ginger or dried cranberries etc.
75g walnuts or pecans, chopped

Put the chocolate, butter, brandy or coffee, caster sugar and vanilla essence into a saucepan over a gentle heat until the butter and chocolate have melted into a runny, smooth mixture. Mix the crushed digestives, the sultanas and the nuts into the melted mixture, stirring well. Pour the mixture into a lined loaf tin and leave to cool - if you can.

Amanda Mackintosh
SHERBORNE, DORSET

Chocolate Nut Slice

250g Bourneville chocolate
200g condensed milk
60g toasted hazelnuts – skinned
60g pecan nuts
60g flaked or whole almonds or pistachios

Melt the chocolate then add the nuts and the milk. Place in a small lined loaf tin. Leave to harden. Turn out and slice thinly when needed.

Janey Heaney
MUCKART, CLACKMANNANSHIRE

Bramble Orange & Almond Cake

275g butter
275g caster sugar
400g self-raising flour
One and a half teaspoons baking powder
5 eggs
Grated rind of 1 orange
1 teaspoon vanilla extract
5 tablespoons milk
275g brambles
37g flaked almonds

Glacé Icing
150g icing sugar
1 teaspoon vanilla extract
2 tablespoons juice from the orange

Preheat oven to 190°C, gas mark 5. Line a baking tray 30cm x 20cm with greaseproof paper. Cream butter and sugar, sift in flour, baking powder, then add eggs, orange zest, milk, & vanilla. Beat until light and fluffy. Fold in the brambles, then sprinkle almonds on top. Bake for 40-45 minutes. Cool the cake then ice with the Glace Orange Vanilla icing.

Carolyne Charrington
TRESHNISH, ISLE OF MULL

Carrot Cake

2 cups flour
1 and a half cups caster sugar
1 teaspoon baking powder
1 teaspoon baking soda
1 and a half teaspoons cinnamon
4 eggs
1 and a quarter cups sunflower oil
2 cups packed grated carrot
– plus a little more

Icing
175g butter
225g Philadelphia cheese
2 teaspoons vanilla essence
500g icing sugar

Preheat oven to 180°C, gas mark 4.
Sift all dry ingredients. Beat eggs and oil
together. Add to dry ingredients together
with grated carrots - mix lightly with a spoon.
Bake in two well greased 23cm cake tins for
40 minutes, cool and then sandwich them
together with the icing.

To make the icing
Soften butter, mix all the ingredients
together until smooth. Happy baking!

Caroline Pelly
ABOYNE, ABERDEENSHIRE

Charlie's Malteser Cake

Not the healthiest but definitely the most
tasty! Good in squares at afternoon tea or
cut into slices to accompany a pudding
– try Easy Lemon Syllabub on page 152.

100g margarine
6 tablespoons golden syrup
250g cooking chocolate
200g crushed digestive biscuits – best kept
in small chunks with as little crumbs as
possible
200g crushed maltesers - best done while
still in the packet, and add a few whole
ones to it

Melt the margarine, syrup and chocolate
over a low heat. When it's all melted, take off
the heat and add the crushed biscuits and
maltesers. Mix really well. Spread into a lined
greased loaf tin. Chill in the fridge then cut
up into slices. Keep refrigerated. This can
also be frozen.

Charlie Drysdale
KILRIE, FIFE

TIP...
If you are ever stuck in the middle
of nowhere and need the times of buses,
or perhaps you want to know what is on
at the local cinema or even how many calories
you would burn by walking to the moon
— just text AQA ('any questions answered')
to 63336 and they will answer
within about 10 minutes
(costs £1 a shot)

Cheat's ten-minute Strawberry Gateau

SERVES 4/6

1 x 25Og sponge flan case
600ml double cream
25g caster sugar
2 tablespoons (approximately) brandy
1 and a half 250g punnets strawberries
55g icing sugar
Few sprigs fresh mint

Spun-sugar topping
175g caster sugar

Cut out the centre of the flan, using a 20-25cm stainless-steel ring (or the ring of a spring-form cake tin, without the base). With a sharp knife, carefully cut this sponge disc in half through the middle so you end up with two thin discs. Place the ring on a surface or tray, and put one of the discs inside it.

Whip the double cream with the sugar and brandy until thick. Keep in the fridge. Hull the strawberries. Leave some whole for a garnish (about ten of the small ones). Cut the rest in half lengthways. Line the ring with the largest strawberry halves with the cut side against the ring. You won't need all of them at this stage. Spoon the chilled, whipped cream into the ring and gently press to the edges, keeping the strawberries in place against the sides. Arrange the rest of the halved strawberries over the top. Add the other sponge disc, and press it down.

Dust generously with icing sugar. Lift the cake on to a plate. Remove the ring by carefully warming the edges with a hot cloth and lifting it straight off.

Place the sugar for the spun-sugar into a very clean pan and heat. Once caramelised – golden brown and sizzling – remove from the heat to cool slightly. While this is cooling, take a metal skewer and hold it in a gas flame until it is red hot. Use it to score the top of the gateau in lines to create a diamond pattern. Decorate the top with the left-over strawberries and berries and garnish with sprigs of fresh mint. To finish, dip a small spoon into the caramelised sugar and twist it around a steel to create some sugar curls. Continue doing this until you have a candyfloss texture. Place this on top of the berries and serve.

Nick Nairn
NICK NAIRN COOK SCHOOL – PORT OF MENTEITH, STIRLING

Charlotte's Brownies

Half a cup oil
3 and a half cups sugar
4 eggs
1 teaspoon vanilla
2 cups flour
1 and a third cups unsweetened cocoa – divided
Boiling water – approx one third of a cup
Chocolate chips – approx 1 cup

Preheat oven to 180°C, Gas Mark 4.
Grease 23cm x 33cm or 25cm X 35cm tray.
Pour boiling water over a third cup of cocoa and mix well. Let it sit while you do the rest.
Beat the oil and sugar together. Beat in the eggs and add the vanilla. Next, stir in the flour – the batter will be stiff. Pour in the water and cocoa mixture and mix together. Add the remaining cup of cocoa and mix in. Add all the chocolate chips. Spread the mixture into a tray and bake for 25-30 minutes.
Note: you may skip the boiling water and cocoa stage, and just mix in the cocoa with batter, but it isn't as tasty!

Charlotte Blau
UNIVERSITY OF DUNDEE MEDICAL SCHOOL

Cheese Biscuits

Equal quantities of the following:
Flour
Strongest Cheddar cheese you can get
Margarine – cut up
Pinch of mustard powder & cayenne pepper – these 2 items are not compulsory!

Preheat oven to 180°C, gas mark 4.
Put the flour and margarine into a food processor. When it looks like breadcrumbs take it out and put it in to a bowl. Add the grated cheese and mix together with the mustard and cayenne if using.
Roll out on floured board not too thinly and then cut out to whatever shape you like. Brush the tops with beaten egg or milk . Bake in the oven for approx 20 minutes but keep an eye on them as cheese can burn ! Take great care when removing from cooking tray as these are fragile. Don't eat them all at once but they are very moreish.

Sabrina Humphrey
DINNET, ABERDEENSHIRE

Cheese Muffins

MAKES 6

1 cup flour
3 teaspoons baking powder
1 and a half cups grated cheese
Quarter teaspoon mustard
Half teaspoon salt
1 egg
3 quarters of a cup milk

Preheat oven to 200°C, gas mark 6.
Sift the flour with the baking powder and add the cheese, mustard and salt. Beat the egg in a cup and fill to the brim with milk. Add to the dry ingredients mixing thoroughly. Divide mixture into a well greased muffin tin and bake for 10 mins.

Caroline Pelly
ABOYNE, ABERDEENSHIRE

Christmas Pudding Petit Fours

I have given this recipe to many people and I have made a batch every Christmas for the last 10 years. They always disappear at great speed... It is unbelievably easy to do and looks really classy .

1 block of ready-made dark fruit cake about 20cm by 10cm
2 dessertspoons sherry or brandy
1 dessertspoon orange cordial
Block of white cooking chocolate
Glacé cherries
Angelica
Petits four cases

Crumble the fruit cake into a bowl. Add the orange cordial. Add the sherry or brandy and mix into a stiff paste. Roll the mixture into small balls (1 heaped teaspoon per ball) which will fit into the petit four cases. Put the balls into the fridge to chill.
    Break up the white chocolate and melt it gently in a bowl over a pan of boiling water. Drop a teaspoonful over each of the balls so that the effect is of sauce over a Christmas pudding. Chop up the glacé cherries and angelica and put one piece of red and one of green onto each 'pudding' to decorate. Put them back into the fridge to chill for at least 4 hours. They can then be put into a storage tin or box and will last the festive season.
    A friend of mine has a husband who does not like fruit cake and she makes a super variation using Jamaica Ginger cake instead of the fruit cake.

Dr Jane Mackay
BASICS EDUCATION SCOTLAND, INVERNESS

Dark Gingerbread

225g butter
225g dark brown sugar
225g black treacle
2 large free-range eggs
340g plain flour – I use half whole-wheat
2 heaped teaspoons ground ginger
1 teaspoon ground cinnamon
2 teaspoons bicarbonate of soda dissolved in 280ml warm milk

Preheat oven to 170°C, gas mark 3. Line a loaf tin with baking parchment. Melt the butter, sugar and treacle together in a pan. Allow the mixture to cool until barely warm, then beat in the eggs. Sift in the flour, ginger and cinnamon and stir into the treacle mixture. Stir the milk mixture into the cake mixture. Pour the thin batter into the loaf tin and bake for about 40 minutes.

Jo Stover
ALFORD, ABERDEENSHIRE

Tablet

900g granulated sugar
50g butter
Large tin condensed milk
425ml milk

Dissolve the sugar in the milk and bring to the boil. Boil for 15 minutes. Add the condensed milk and boil for a further 5 minutes. Stir well and pour into a greased tin. When cool cut into squares.

Mrs Robb
CRATHES, KINCARDINESHIRE

Delicious Chocolate Cake

SERVES 8

2 x 100g bars of really good
dark chocolate
200g unsalted butter
140g caster sugar or 110g fructose
6 egg yolks
8 egg whites

Preheat oven to 160°C, gas mark 3.
Butter a 25cm springform or loose-based
cake tin. Melt the chocolate and the butter
in a bowl over a pan of simmering water.
Remove from the heat and set it aside.
    Put the sugar or fructose into a bowl and
whisk together with the egg yolks until thick
and pale. Pour into the melted chocolate
and mix together until smooth. Whisk the
egg whites until they form soft peaks.
Gently fold these into the chocolate mixture
until it's well mixed. Pour into the cake tin
and bake for 45 minutes.
    If you want a more mousse-like cake
take 10 minutes off the cooking time. It will
rise up during cooking and sink alarmingly
when you take it out but that's fine. Leave
to cool. Dust with icing sugar. This cake is
delicious with berries and crème fraiche It
keeps well in the fridge for a few days.

Bev Remp
INVERURIE, ABERDEENSHIRE

Cornflake Cookies

40g butter
40g sugar
60g cornflakes
1 tablespoon golden syrup
25g cocoa

Melt the butter, sugar and golden syrup in
large saucepan. Mix in the cocoa and
cornflakes. Put in paper cases or in dollops
on a baking tray. Allow to cool and harden.

Mo Farquharson
WHITEHOUSE, ABERDEENSHIRE

'Dougie Biscuits'

If your child goes stratospheric on sugar, as
many of ours do, then give them biscuits
that have no added sugar in them as snacks.
The following are known as 'Dougie Biscuit's'
in our family. My eldest son used to go
berserk on sugar (still does – you should see
him on Coke. It is like spinach and Popeye)
so these were invented/found for him.

75g margarine or butter
175g malt extract
250g chopped dates
250g porridge oats
Plus seeds, nuts, chopped ginger, dried
apricots, anything or nothing more.
The dates are vital as they help stick
everything together.

Preheat oven to 200°C, gas mark 6.
Melt the butter in a pan and combine all
ingredients. Spread the mixture in a tray
about half an inch thick and press down.
Bake for 15 minutes. Cut into squares.

Rob Wainwright
ISLE OF COLL
FORMER SCOTLAND RUGBY CAPTAIN AND BRITISH LION

Fail-me-never Gingerbread

110g margarine
2 tablespoons syrup and 2 tablespoons treacle mixed
2 eggs
1 teaspoon mixed spice
1 teaspoon ginger
1 tea cup brown sugar
2 tea cups plain flour
1 small cup hot water

Preheat oven to 190C, gas mark 5. Cream the margarine and sugar. Add the syrup and the treacle. Beat in the eggs. Fold in the flour and spices. Dissolve the bicarbonate of soda in the hot water then stir into the mixture and pour into a prepared baking loaf tin. Bake for 40-45 minutes.

Mrs Robb
CRATHES, KINCARDINESHIRE

Flapjacks

MAKES 8/10

75g butter or block margarine
50g light soft brown sugar
30ml (2 level tablespoons) golden syrup
175g rolled oats

Preheat oven to 180°C, gas mark 4. Grease a shallow 18cm square cake tin. Melt the butter with the sugar and syrup and mix together with the rolled oats. Turn into the prepared tin and press down well. Bake in the oven for about 20 minutes, until golden brown. Cool slightly and then mark into fingers with sharp knife and loosen around edges. Remove from tin when firm.

Harry Maitland
CRATHES, KINCARDINESHIRE

Foolproof Scones

MAKES 8/9

175g self raising wholemeal flour
175g self raising white flour
75g soft butter or margarine
Pinch of salt
175ml milk

Preheat oven to 200°C, gas mark 6. Gently rub the fat into the flour and salt, gradually add the milk and mix with a flat knife. Gently kneed with your hands - don't over mix. Roll out the dough thickly (about 3cm in depth) and use a scone cutter 6cm in diameter to form 8 to 9 scones. Place on a lightly buttered heavy weight baking tray and place in the centre of oven for 10 minutes or until well risen and lightly brown. These are especially good served with lemon curd and a dollop of thick Greek yogurt.

Letitia Smith-Bumett
KEMNAY, ABERDEENSHIRE

Granny's Chocolate Brownies

This brownie recipe is from my granny who discovered it when she was in America working on her PhD. She was there during prohibition, so they drank their whisky from china teacups. Green & Black's organic cocoa powder is amazing in this recipe.

100g butter
38g cocoa
2 eggs
225g caster sugar
50g self raising flour
50g – 100g walnuts
1 teaspoon vanilla essence

Preheat oven to 180°C, gas mark 4. Grease and line a shallow cake tin. Melt the butter in a saucepan and add the cocoa (you can bung it all in together and leave on a gentle heat while you beat the eggs). Beat the eggs and sugar until light and creamy. Add cocoa/butter mixture, vanilla essence, chopped nuts and fold in the flour. Pour into tin and bake for 30 minutes.

   You can leave out the nuts and it's still delicious. Cut into small pieces (it's very rich) and sieve a little icing sugar on top. It looks like snow on a fresh mole hill.

Steve and Kate Redpath
TARLAND, ABERDEENSHIRE

Highland Shortbread

225g plain flour
55g cornflour
110g farola or semolina
150g caster sugar
110g butter
110g margarine
Demerara sugar for coating

Preheat oven to 160°C, gas mark 2-3. Cream all the ingredients together. Roll into a big sausage 4cm thick, coat with demerara sugar on the outside edge. Slice into 1cm rounds. Space them out on your baking tray and bake in oven for approx 20 minutes.

Mrs Robb
CRATHES, KINCARDINESHIRE

Iron Will Cake

50g butter
25g soft brown sugar
125g dates – mashed
2 lightly beaten eggs
125g grated carrot
175 self raising wholemeal flour
1 teaspoon ground cinnamon
25g flax seeds
25g raisins
125ml milk

Preheat oven to 180°C, gas mark 4. Line a cake tin with baking parchment. Cream the butter and sugar and mix in the dates, egg, carrot and cinnamon. Sift the flour and fold into the mixture with the seeds and raisins, adding the milk gradually. Spoon into the tin. Bake for about 45 minutes or until golden. Test if it's ready by piercing with a skewer: if it comes out clean its done!

Laurie Mill
METHVEN, PERTHSHIRE

Squashed Fly Squares!

225g butter
225g self raising flour
225g caster sugar
450g sultanas or raisins
2 eggs beaten

Preheat oven to 180°C, gas mark 4.
Melt the butter and sugar in a pan until the sugar has dissolved. Add the rest of the ingredients and put into a lined baking tray in the centre of the oven for about 20 minutes – no longer. Leave to stand in the baking tray until cooled a bit. Turn out and cut into squares. Try not to eat it all at once!

Miranda McHardy
BANCHORY, KINCARDINESHIRE

Leys Truffles

MAKES 12 /16 TRUFFLES

400g dark chocolate
1 egg
5 tablespoons double cream
A generous slug of brandy
Chocolate powder to roll truffles in
– dark or milk

Melt the chocolate and cream in a bowl over hot water. Take off the heat and whisk in the egg and brandy. Leave to cool.
   Scoop out a full teaspoon of chocolate mixture, roll into a ball, then into the chocolate powder. Store in the fridge - unless you eat them all at once!

Vinnie Burnett
CRATHES, BANCHORY

Monique's Gateau au Chocolat

SERVES 8 GENEROUSLY

5 large eggs
250g caster sugar
250g best dark chocolate – eg Meunier, Lindt, Valrhona
110 g unsalted butter
5 dessertspoons plain flour

Preheat oven to 160°C, gas mark 2-3.
Prepare a 25 cm cake tin, not too deep and not with a loose bottom as the cake will ooze out. Grease and line the bottom with baking parchment.
   Melt the chocolate and butter together gently in a bowl over barely simmering water. Cool. Whisk the eggs and sugar until thick and frothy. Add the cooled chocolate mixture to the egg mixture and stir well to combine. Fold in the flour and pour into the prepared tin. Bake for 20 to 25 minutes then remove from oven and allow to cool completely in the tin before attempting to turn the cake out.
   This cake should not be overcooked as it is supposed to be very moist. Before serving, dust with icing sugar and accompany with fresh berries and whipped cream.

Gillian Vieilledent
LUMPHANAN, ABERDEENSHIRE

Mrs Rock's Pancakes

225g self-raising flour
Half a teaspoon baking soda
Three quarters teaspoon cream of tartar
Three tablespoons sugar
2 eggs, beaten
Milk
Half a tablespoon olive oil

Sieve the flour into a mixing bowl and add baking soda, cream of tartar and sugar. Mix well and make a hole in the middle. Put the beaten eggs into the mixture and mix into the dry ingredients, also adding some milk. Mix to a thick pouring consistency, not too runny. Add the olive oil and mix in. Spoon the mixture (3 or 4 dollops!) onto the hot plate of an AGA/Rayburn or onto a fairly hot griddle (greased with butter). Once there are bubbles forming turn over and cook on the other side. Transfer onto a wire wrack with a clean tea towel on it, cover to keep warm.

Lisa Hector
ALYTH, PERTHSHIRE

Raisin Drops

Marvellous to make with children and tastes so much better than cardboard shop biscuits.

75g of sugar
225g of self raising flour
100g margarine
15ml milk
Half cup of raisins
15ml syrup
5ml of bicarbonate of soda

Preheat oven to 180°C, gas mark 4. Put the sugar, syrup, margarine and milk into a pan and heat but do not boil. Mix in the bicarbonate and stir until it froths up. Now take it off the hob. Tip the flour into a bowl and throw in the raisins. Add the flour and raisins into the frothing mixture. Stir well until the mixture leaves the side of the pan. Put sixteen teaspoon-sized dollops of the mixture, well spaced out, on a greased baking tray and bake for 15 minutes or so. Take out and cool on a wire rack.

Lucy Gordon
OLDMELDRUM, ABERDEENSHIRE

Ra's Cocoa Cake

450g caster sugar
250g plain flour
150g cocoa
One and a half teaspoons
bicarbonate of soda
One and half teaspoons baking powder
Pinch of salt
2 eggs
100ml corn oil
180ml milk
2 teaspoons vanilla essence
180mls boiling water

Cocoa Icing
100g soft butter
60g cocoa
350g icing sugar
100ml milk
1 teaspoon vanilla

Preheat oven to 180°C, gas mark 4.

Combine dry ingredients in bowl, add eggs, milk, oil, vanilla, beat 2 minutes.

Stir in boiling water (batter is thin). Place in 23cm high sided cake tin. Cook 35 minutes - or 'til done. To make icing, cream butter, add cocoa, sugar and then the milk slowly. Beat. Add vanilla. Spread on cake and EAT! It's a very squodgy cake and keeps well.

David and Susie Hawson
MONYMUSK, ABERDEENSHIRE

Lemon Drizzle Cake

350g butter
350g soft brown sugar
350g self raising flour
4 eggs – beaten
Grated rind of 2 lemons

Drizzle
Juice of 2 lemons
225g caster sugar

Preheat oven to 180°C, gas mark 4. Melt the butter and sugar, then beat in the flour, eggs and lemon rind. Divide between two lined loaf tins and bake for 25 – 30 minutes until skewer comes out clean.

Leave to cool in tin slightly before adding drizzle. Leave until completely cold before cutting into slices. This cake will keep well for a week in an airtight tin.

Catheryn Huntly
ABOYNE, KINCARDINESHIRE

Sticky Marmalade Loaf

One third of 454g jar of marmalade (chunky is good)
175g softened butter
175g muscovado sugar
3 eggs beaten
225g self-raising flour
Half a teaspoon baking powder
2 teaspoons ground ginger
1 teaspoon mixed spice
100g pecan halves

Preheat oven to 180°C, gas mark 4. Line a 1kg loaf tin. Set aside one tablespoon of marmalade in a small pan. Blend all ingredients (except the nuts) until smooth and light. Stir in three quarters of the nuts. Put the mixture in the loaf tin and sprinkle on the remaining nuts. Bake for one to one and a quarter hours until a skewer comes out clean. Heat the reserved marmalade and spread over top of warm loaf.

Caroline Gilchrist
DORNOCH, SUTHERLAND

Sugary Apple Muffins
MAKES 12

A great family favourite!

100g self raising flour
50g margarine
50g caster sugar
75g finely chopped apple
1 egg
1 teaspoon baking powder
Pinch of cinnamon

Pinch of nutmeg
1 tablespoon milk
12 baking cases

Preheat oven to 220°C, gas mark 7.
Cream the margarine and sugar together.
Beat in the egg. Mix the flour, baking powder
and spices and fold in with the milk to
creamed mixture. Fold in the apple and fill 12
baking cases with the mixture. Sprinkle an
extra bit of caster sugar and spices over the
tops if liked. Bake for about 15 minutes.

Lorna McGuire
ST CYRUS, ANGUS

Syrup Ginger Buns

100g margarine
100g caster sugar
150g golden syrup
1 egg
200g plain flour
Half teaspoon mixed spice
1 level teaspoon ground ginger
Half level teaspoon bicarbonate of soda
142 ml water – warm
1 – 2 tablespoons finely chopped
preserved ginger

Preheat oven to 190°C, gas mark 5.
Cream/beat together the margarine, syrup
and sugar until light and fluffy. Gradually
beat in the egg. Sieve the flour with the spice
and ginger. Blend the bicarbonate of soda
with the warm water (not boiling). Stir half of
the flour into the mixture, mix and then stir in
half of the liquid and mix. Repeat. Add the

chopped ginger and mix. Place 20 paper
cases on either a flat tray or in bun tins. Half
fill each paper case with the mixture. Bake
for 15 - 20 minutes until golden brown and
firm to the touch.

June Scott
LORETTO SCHOOL, EAST LOTHIAN

South African Mielie Bread (or Corn Bread)
Delicious with a BBQ

2 cups flour
3 teaspoons baking powder
1 teaspoon salt
2 extra large eggs – beaten
1 cup grated cheddar cheese
75ml milk
1 can cream style sweetcorn

Preheat oven to 180°C, gas mark 4.
Mix all the ingredients together. Bake in a
small loaf tin for 45 minutes.

Sue Buchan
BRIDGE OF CALLY, PERTHSHIRE

TIP...
Use egg whites
from older eggs
for meringues,
they will be
fluffier

The no-mixer-I-can't-be-bothered-it's-too-difficult Chocolate Cake

275g self-raising flour
225g caster sugar
One and a half teaspoons baking powder
200g mayonnaise
margarine
One teaspoon vanilla essence
4 tablespoons cocoa powder
250ml water

Preheat oven to 180°C, gas mark 4. Grease a baking tin with some margarine. Any shape of tin will do, but if circular, use a tin which is at least 18 cm in diameter and has quite high sides.

Mix the flour, sugar and baking powder together in a bowl with a spoon. Add the mayonnaise and mix gently – don't beat it. Continue until the mixture looks like breadcrumbs in texture. (This won't take you very long or use up much energy!)
Add the vanilla essence, cocoa powder and water, and continue to mix gently with the spoon until the mixture is smooth.

Pour the mixture into the tin and bake in the oven for about an hour. A good test to see if a cake is ready is to put a clean knife into the thickest part of the cake. If it comes out clean, then the cake is ready. If there is some mixture on the knife, leave the cake for another few minutes, then test again. Leave the cake to cool in the tin for about 10 minutes. Loosen it by sliding a knife around the sides and then it should come out reasonably easily onto a plate.

Diana Murdoch
LARGO, FIFE

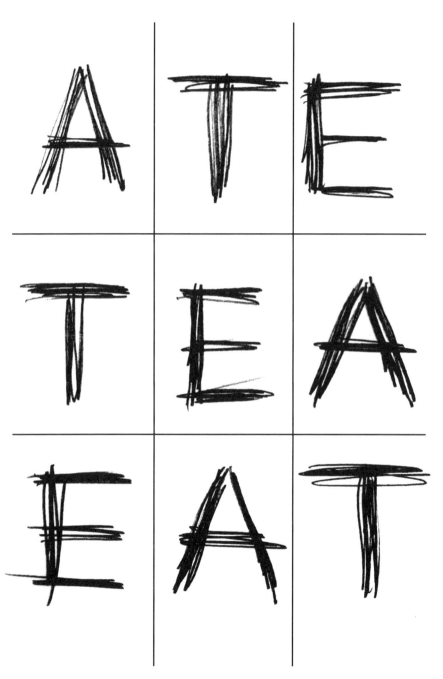

after Alan Fletcher

drinks

Drink (drink) *vb.*
drinks,drinking,
drank, drunk
1. To swallow (a liquid);
imbibe. **2**. (*tr.*) to take in or
soak up (liquid); absorb:

Pureed Strawberry Prosecco

One and a quarter cups frozen sliced strawberries with sugar, thawed (you can use fresh)
1 x 750ml bottle Prosecco – chilled
6 small strawberries to decorate

Purée sliced strawberries and any juice in a blender. Press the mixture through a sieve into a bowl to remove any seeds. Chill for thirty minutes. Combine strawberry purée and Prosecco in a large pitcher and gently stir to mix. Pour into 6 champagne flutes. Decorate rim of glass with a sliced strawberry. Serve.

Lisa Bain
ABERDEEN

Fresh Lemon Squash

3 lemons
225g granulated sugar
Water

Chop the lemons into chunks and put in blender or food processor with the sugar. Fill up to the 1 litre mark with cold water. Blend until mushy, then sieve into a large jug. Put the bits of mushy lemon back into blender/food processor and fill up again with cold water to 1 litre mark. Blend again and sieve the mixture into the jug. Taste to see if it is sweet enough and if necessary, add more sugar. Chill and serve.

Verity Walters
ALFORD, ABERDENSHIRE

Five Minute Smoothie

1 ripe banana
150g red fruit (raspberries, strawberries, blackberries etc or a mixture)
Apple Juice
Runny honey to serve

Slice the banana into a blender. Add the berries of your choice. Whizz until smooth. With blades still turning, pour in the apple juice (or water) to make to required consistency. Pour into a glass, toss a few extra fruits on top, drizzle with honey and serve.

You could use melon or a slightly over-ripe mango instead of the banana – or add a pot of low fat natural yogurt to make an extra creamy smoothie.

Noelle Fyffe
FETTERNEAR, ABERDEENSHIRE

Warming Winter Punch

SERVES 6

1 large orange
300ml rum or brandy
2 tablespoons soft brown sugar
50g blanched almonds
6 cloves
1 bottle red wine
300ml orange juice
50g raisins
1 cinnamon stick

Stick the orange with cloves and place in a saucepan. Add all the other ingredients. Leave to stand for about 30 minutes, or longer if possible. Then, very slowly, heat the punch, keeping the heat on the lowest setting. When the punch has had time to reach full flavour (about 30 to 40 minutes), serve very warm.

Audrey Moore
BADACHRO, WESTER ROSS

Robin's Christmas Special

SERVES 6

An easy way to liven up a cocktail party. You can use a demi-sec or decent sparkling wine as an alternative to champagne – if it's for your mother-in-law.

75ml cranberry juice
100ml champagne
12.5ml Cointreau

For Christmas style, you have to prepare the glasses first. Mix white granulated sugar with pink food colouring, then pour some Cointreau into a saucer. Take each glass and dip it (upside down preferably) into the Cointreau and then into the pink sugar. Allow the pink sugar rim to dry before pouring the cocktail.

Pour cranberry juice into a champagne flute and fill with champagne. Top with a float of Cointreau.

Robin Maitland
CRATHES, KINCARDINESHIRE

Elderflower Cordial

24 elderflower heads (bug-free!)
3 lemons – quartered
75g tartaric or citric acid
2kg sugar
1.1 litre boiling water

Put all the ingredients in a large, deep casserole dish – slightly squeeze lemon quarters into water before adding. Stir well, once a day for 3-5 days. Strain, bottle and chill.

Biddy Wood
LAMBERHURST, KENT

Two Summer Smoothies

EACH MAKES 2

Groovy Smoothie
1 small banana
6 strawberries and or raspberries
– or any fresh fruit
2 big tablespoons yogurt or Galloway ice cream

It Takes 2 to Mango
– for 2, from one glass perhaps
1 small banana
200ml cloudy apple juice
2 heaped tablespoons sheep's yogurt
6 chunks fresh or tinned mango

For both above, liquidise and drink immediately!

Jane Lorimer
LEVEN, FIFE

Jack's Smoothies

Summer Whizz
2 handfuls of strawberries
2 nectarines
1 banana
5 tablespoons natural yoghurt

Whizz together and decorate with chopped strawberries

Tropical Ice Smoothie
1 bag of frozen tropical fruit smoothie mix (available from the supermarket)
1 large tub of natural yoghurt
Honey to sweeten if necessary

Whizz together to make a delicious thick smoothie with icy fruit crystals.

Jackoberry Sparkle
2 handfuls of strawberries
2 handfuls of blueberries
5 ice cubes
Sparkling water

Whizz together strawberries, blueberries and ice cubes. Top up with sparkling water. A wonderfully refreshing drink for a warm sunny day.

Jack Maitland,
CRATHES, KINCARDINESHIRE

Non-Alcoholic Cocktail – but tastes alcoholic!

Mix half tonic water or soda water with half fresh orange juice and add a few drops of Angostura bitters. Mmmmm – refreshing. Don't forget the ice!

Nicky Forbes
ALFORD, ABERDEENSHIRE

Low Fat Raspberry Smoothie

275ml skimmed milk
1 small carton 0% fat yogurt
Handful of raspberries

Whizz fruit, milk and yogurt in blender for 30 – 45 seconds.

Val Rahtz
ECHT, ABERDEENSHIRE

Coupe Colonel!

PER PERSON

2 scoops lime sorbet
2 shots vodka

Serve in an interesting glass with a spoon and watch them swoon.

Gillian Vieilledent
LUMPHANAN, ABERDEENSHIRE

Three Yummy Cocktails

Silver Shower
Totally delicious and very gulp-able!

40ml White Rum
15ml Falurnum (if available)
Pineapple Juice
Lime Juice

Green Monkey
A cocktail named after the very special
Green Monkey Golf course at Sandy Lane,
where even the bunkers are cut in the shape
of the green monkeys that abound over the
course.

40ml White Rum
15ml Melon Liqueur
Golden Apple Juice
Passion fruit Juice

Swedish Tiger Rose
We can take this as Tiger Woods'
contribution to The Sandpiper Cookbook.
The cocktail was created for the wedding of
Tiger Woods to Swedish model Elin
Nordegren in October 2004. As the wedding
cost a reputed $1.5m this is an exclusive
cocktail indeed!

One and a half measure of Absolut
Mandarin
One and a half measure of Apricot Brandy
1 dash Curacao
Pineapple Juice
Orange Juice

Sandy Lane Country Club
BARBADOS

When asked by Claire Maitland for his
favourite cocktail, Sir Garry Sobers replied;
'It's plain and simple:
Scotch On The Rocks'

Sir Garry Sobers
WEST INDIES CRICKETING LEGEND - BARBADOS

...and more

Toffee Vodka
Put a whole bag of Werther's Originals
into a bottle of vodka and screw the
cap back on. Put the bottle into
the dishwasher for the longest
hottest cycle.

Lanrick Bramble Whisky
l litre whisky
450g of brambles
325 g sugar

Place ingredients into a large bottle or
demijohn and turn every week until all the
sugar has dissolved. The longer you leave
it the better.

Margaritas
1 shot of Tequila
1 shot of Cointreau
Juice of one lime (if particularly sour,
add a little sugar or sugar syrup)

Salt glasses and pour over crushed ice.

Simon Dickson
DOUNE, PERTHSHIRE

A Well Winter Elderberry Syrup

Black elderberries
450g of sugar for 575ml juice
10 cloves

On a dry day, go back to all those elderflower you didn't get round to picking for cordial this summer and pick them as heads of ripe, black elderberries instead. Wash and drain well. Strip berries from stalks, place in pan and just cover with water. Simmer until fruit is very soft (about 30 minutes). Strain through jelly bag/muslin and measure juice. Allow 450g sugar and 10 cloves for each 575ml juice. Gently heat berry juice with cloves, stirring in sugar until it has dissolved. Boil for 10 minutes. Remove from the heat and leave to stand until completely cold.

This can be frozen in easily usable small quantities or stored in small mixer glass bottles (sterilised).

Use as a diluted (2 tablespoons) hot drink, with a squeeze of lemon. It will bring on a sweat, stop a cold and relieve chestiness. It's good with whisky – the ultimate hot toddy. Use the syrup recipe for ripe blackcurrants and combine the two as a delicious hot drink remedy with all that extra Vitamin C.

Virginia Irvine-Fortescue
BALFRON, STIRLINGSHIRE

Orange Gin

4 Seville oranges
450g sugar
300ml water
l.l litres gin

I use Seville oranges because they are much sharper tasting than normal oranges. Boil sugar with water and leave to cool. Grate the peel off the oranges by putting cling film over the finest part of your grater and grate the oranges on this. You can then collect off all the grating easily making sure not to grate the white pith. Put all the gratings into the sugar syrup mixture and pour into bottle along with the gin. Shake gently over two weeks, leaving in kitchen. Then strain liquid through fine plastic sieve or muslin and store for about six months before drinking. (You could add a couple of coffee beans once strained.)

Penny Dickson
DOUNE, PERTHSHIRE

'The Golden Hour'

Mix and sip on a warm Scottish summer evening – *you'll be lucky*.

35ml vodka – ice cold
50ml grape juice
10ml lemon juice
5ml elderflower cordial
3 mint leaves
3 basil leaves
Garnish with lemon spirals

The Maitlands
CRATHES, KINCARDINESHIRE

Cheat's Sangria

1 bottle of red wine
Half a bottle of Lemon Fanta
Garnish with sliced oranges and lemons.

it's that simple...

The Maitlands
CRATHES, KINCARDINESHIRE

Sloe Gin

Frankly, as they don't grow up here no-one
does it better than Mr Gordons (rather like
Mr Birds Eye & his peas!) but have found this
from long memory...
    Pick sloes wearing thick gloves (if after
first frost they might not need 'pricking').
Freeze to burst skins. In sterile glass
bottles/containers add same weight as sloes
in sugar (cubes is easiest!) and top up until
ALMOST full with gin of choice. Shake
occasionally for at least 2 months then strain
and decant into sterile glass bottles & date!

Kate Nicolson
CAIRNBULG, ABERDEENSHIRE

Nine 'til Five

SERVES 4 (MAKES ABOUT 450ML)

This is a Holtum family speciality. Hard day
at work, school (over 18 of course!) or on
the cricket pitch – grab one of these and
just relax!

275ml of cranberry juice
150ml of bitter lemon

2 to 3 (depending what sort of day it's
been!) tablespoons of dark rum
 Ice cubes to serve

Mix all ingredients together in a large jug.
Pour into glasses with ice.

Jamie Holtum
NEWCASTLE UNIVERSITY

Horse's Neck

This is an old naval drink and the perfect
reviver on a Sunday morning after a heavy
Saturday night. For some reason it tastes
best out of half pint pewter mugs but any
half pint glass will do.

Half fill the mug with ice cubes and add 3 or
4 good sloshes of Angostura Bitters. Add a
generous measure of Cape Brandy from
South Africa such as KWV (VS) which only
costs about £10 a bottle. If you haven't got
this then use a very expensive cognac.
Cheap French brandies will not do. Fill to the
brim with Schweppes' Original Dry Ginger if
you can find it (which I can't). Next best is
Tesco's own brand Dry Ginger. Add a good
wedge of lemon.
    Drink two of these and you will feel well
refreshed! It is a delicious drink.

Allan Macpherson-Fletcher
BALAVIL, INVERNESS-SHIRE

Lavender's Healthy Lunch Drink

Half jar Libby's tomato juice
1 small plain yogurt
Worcestershire sauce to taste
Salt and pepper

Whisk up all the ingredients and serve with oatcakes or toast.

Lavender Maitland
FORFAR, ANGUS

Bloody Mary

Dash of sherry, horseradish and V8 juice (rather than tomato juice), vodka and lime makes the best Bloody Mary.

Vinnie Burnett
CRATHES, KINCARDINESHIRE

Grandpa's Iced Coffee

1 heaped teaspoonful instant coffee
1 spoonful of hot water
Milk
Ice cubes

Dissolve coffee with hot water and put in glass. Fill glass half with milk and top up with ice cubes. Delicious at teatime on a warm sunny day.

John Drysdale
NEWTONMORE, INVERNESS-SHIRE

Clara

One part lager to one part Fanta Lemon. Serve very cold – preferably wearing a bikini!

Bev Remp
INVERURIE, ABERDEENSHIRE

The Sandpiper bag has quite literally been a lifesaver. Thank you.

GP, Orkney

index

b

Beef

Biscuits

Breakfast

Bread

c

Cakes and Baking

Soups

Butternut soup - easy yummy **24**
Cold soup **32**
Cold summer soup **21**
Courgette soup **26**
Crème Taj Mahal **23**
Cucumber vichyssoise **31**
Fish soup – Karelian **26**
French onion soup **25**
Gazpacho with olive bread **20**
Goulash soup **28**
Lentil soup – spicy **27**
Lettuce soup **30**
Mushroom soup – farmhouse **24**
Neep bree **26**
P's big pot of soup **32**
Pea soup **21**
Pea soup – Peterkin's **30**
Pheasant broth – The Hapsburg **25**
Potato soup **31**
Red pepper and tomato soup **21**
Roasted butternut soup with croutons **22**
Root soup **23**
Scotch broth **23**
Smoked haddock chowder **94**
Spring green vitality soup **31**
Sweet potato chilli and coconut soup **21**
Sweet potato soup **27**
Tortellini soup **29**
Vegetable soup – creamed country **28**
Very simple soup **22**
Watercress soup **28**
Wonder plant soup **29**

Starters

Asparagus and egg **35**
Asparagus – baked **34**
Asparagus wrapped in Parma ham **36**
Avocados – grilled with prawns **60**
Baked brie with sun dried tomatoes
    and pine nuts **34**
Camembert – baked with mushrooms,
    pesto and sun dried tomatoes **39**
Camembert – baked with red onion
    marmalade **36**
Camembert en croute **35**
Chicken liver pate **37**
Chicken liver pate with green peppercorns **37**
Dickson's delight **38**
Egg Mousse **34**
Eggs – Prince Youssoupoff's Russian **16**
Goats cheese soufflé **33**
Parmagiana di Melanzane **39**
Mushrooms – baked with Parmesan **33**
Mushrooms – simple garlic **36**
Mushrooms – baked **53**
Mystery starter **37**

Prawns – Chilli and garlic **37**
Red peppers – Italian roasted **35**
Smoked haddock pots **39**
Smoked mackerel pate – cheats **38**
Smoked mackerel pate with melba toast **16**
Smoked salmon pate **33**
Tuna pate **38**

V
Vegetables

Black-eyed Al's Casserole **52**
Carrot and Parsnip Casserole **60**
Courgette fritters **53**
Cabbage – creamy garlic **56**
Potatoes – dauphinoise **55**
Potatoes dauphinoise – quick **53**
Potatoes – Hotch Potch **115**
Red cabbage **62**
Red cabbage – braised **115**
Roast Parsnips **60**

Vegetarian

Asparagus – baked **34**
Aubergine bake **52**
Butternut squash risotto **76**
Couscous and roasted vegetables **57**
Curry sauce recipe **63**
Dahl baht and Tibetan barley bread **58**
Frittata **56**
Goats cheese soufflé **33**
Greek spinach rice – Spanakorizi **56**
Italian roasted red peppers **35**
Lentil salad **43**
Macaroni cheese **75**
Parmigiana di Melanzana **39**
Mushrooms – baked **53**
Pasta sauce – easy **74**
Puy lentil salad **44**
Quiche - onion and mixed vegetable **54**
Quorn enchiladas **62**
Spinach cheese pie **54**
Tagliatelle with broad beans
    and mushrooms **78**
Terkari **58**
Tomato and basil clafoutis **57**
Vegetable couscous **61**
Veggie chilli – Elaine's **60**
White and green stuffed peppers **55**
Wild mushroom risotto **82**
Wild mushrooms baked with Parmesan **33**